Corporate Criminal Liability and Compliance Management Systems

Transnational Crime

Volumes published in this Brill Research Perspective are listed at *brill.com/rptc*

Corporate Criminal Liability and Compliance Management Systems

A Case Study of Spain

By

Santiago Wortman Jofre

BRILL

LEIDEN | BOSTON

Originally published as Volume 2(3) 2018, in *Transnational Crime*, DOI:10.1163/24680931-12340008.

Typeface for the Latin, Greek, and Cyrillic scripts: "Brill". See and download: brill.com/brill-typeface.

ISBN 978-90-04-40773-2 (paperback)
ISBN 978-90-04-40774-9 (e-book)

This book is printed on acid-free paper and produced in a sustainable manner.

Contents

Corporate Criminal Liability and Compliance Management Systems

A Case Study of Spain

Santiago Wortman Jofre
Ph.D. Candidate, Queen Mary University of London
s.wortmanjofre@qmul.ac.uk, santiagowortmanjofre@gmail.com

Abstract

The present work analyses the case of Spain in relation to Compliance Management Systems and Corporate Criminal Liability. It studies the way criminal justice understands and uses Compliance Management Systems to target corporate criminality. Moreover, it aims to deconstruct the way Compliance Management Systems are implemented in different corporations. To that end, I conducted a series of semi-structured interviews with Compliance Officers and performed content analysis on judicial documents. While not being able to generalise or give definite conclusions, the results showed a misconnection between the aim of criminal law provisions and the profit-driven objectives of corporations. Furthermore, results unveiled the powerful motivation of requirements. Companies sought to implement Compliance Management Systems to access new markets, better supplies and insurance fee discounts. Rather than the threat of punishment the analysis indicated a stronger effect through the positive stimuli of requiring a Compliance Management System for a benefit. The study also showed a fear for the reputational consequences of being subjected to a criminal procedure, thus indicating a better predisposition to solve offences through alternative conflict resolution methods. The lack of a clear message from the criminal justice reduced the deterrent effect of punishment. This lack of clear standards may have fostered social disorganisation within the environment of corporations, thus constituting fertile ground for corporate crimes.

Keywords

corporate criminal liability – Compliance Management Systems – corporate criminality – case study – semi-structured interviews – content analysis

 | DOI:10.1163/9789004407749_002

1 Introduction

As Tombs and Whyte (2015, p. 1) pointed out, corporations nowadays manage most of our daily life. We are used to their existence and their relevance in society, thus we normalise and naturalise them even personify them by enduing human characteristics. These features may include from a name to a citizenship, all which help conceptualise the corporations as a gestalt. This personification became a quaint legal construction that enabled the law to address organised business entities (Mark, 1987). Individuals have assigned corporations a specific role in society. People expect organisations to behave in a certain way and obey certain rules. The business logic manages people's most sensitive goods and set the pace of our life. Corporations are mainly profit-driven and that is not always compatible with individual rights.

It has become a cliché to point out the power of corporations. However, the media and citizen watchdogs have alleged several crimes, fines, and abuses by the world's top corporations (The Transnational institute, 2014). Moreover, Wal-Mart Stores revenues in 2013 were more than twice the GDP of countries like Portugal or Ireland (The Transnational institute, 2014). While individuals also have this kind of money-power, they do it through corporations (Dolan & Kroll, 2017).

This generates an awareness of the social impact that wrongful corporate policies can have, perhaps even more than the addition of individual criminal behaviours. The organisational subculture generated by these companies, which interact inside a broader social culture, might serve as fertile ground for criminal behaviours. Corporations are producers of culture: they set norms that are applicable to every employee; they give their staff a sense of membership; they provide a slogan that can be assimilated to national symbols; they set common goals and assign each member a function (McFarland & Gómez, 2014, p. 97). In the words of Thyssen (2009, p. 7), corporations "facilitate communication by providing a shared language and shared themes. At the same time, they offer frameworks for personal identity". The author depicts the idea of cultural insight by stating that when organisations communicate they interweave strategic considerations, that only an insider can understand (Thyssen, 2009, p. 7).

Corporations become something more than the aggregation of its integrating members. The features of personality that society assigns to these fictitious persons provides them with several rights, like the right to own property, citizenship (Hertz Corp. v. Friend et al., 2010; Laufer, 2014, p. 31); and certain obligations, such as paying taxes. This interaction as a normal citizen poses the question of their social responsibility: should they be punished for breaking social norms?

A company that fosters a culture of self-primacy may one day be confronted with the dilemma of behaving against the norms of society to fulfil its goals. In this case, the employee that committed a crime would perhaps not have done so if the Company would not have generated the strain between corporate norms and social laws. In other words, the mores of the corporate subculture do not always share the same goals as the law (Sutherland, 1944, p. 138).

On the other hand, criminal law rises the question: can corporations behave? And if they cannot, how does the criminal justice system justify a punishment for a criminal offence? These questions become particularly relevant since "from the very nature of the organization of a corporation it is apparent that nearly every crime known to the law can be committed by it" (Judge Cicero J. Lindley, 1899, cited in Laufer, 2014, p. 6). However, as it will be shown throughout this work, neither criminological nor criminal law theories have come to a conclusive explanation of the causes and deontological consequences for corporate crime.

1.1 *Research Questions, Hypothesis, and Relevance*

Considering the aforementioned issues, the main two questions discussed in this work are:

- How have Compliance Management Systems (CMSs) been understood and used by the law to target corporate criminality?
- And, how do CMSs work in different corporations?

The main thesis will rely in the failure of achieving a deterrent effect through severer punishments. Yet, criminal law could play a major role in corporate deterrence albeit through the reputational consequence that a criminal procedure implies, as the loss of business opportunities. Thus, Compliance Management Systems may be introduced not only as a preventive mechanism, but as an investment. Regarding this setup, while not being able to draft definitive conclusions, it will be pointed out the effect of unclear judicial acts on corporate behaviours.

In that sense, Compliance Management Systems (CMS) are defined as a "set of interrelated or interacting elements of an organization to establish policies and objectives and processes to achieve those objectives" (International Organization for Standardization, 2014, pp. 2–3). These objectives can be legally imposed or freely chosen, to manage the risk of harming their own reputation (Gasiorowski-Denis, 2014).

As Fleming (2014) points out, the compliance officer position flourished after a "tsunami of regulatory initiatives and substantial fines that followed the financial crisis of 2007–09". Moreover, by pointing out a 2012 speech given by Andy Haldane as head of the financial stability at the Bank of England, Fleming highlighted the European strive to follow the requirements of Basel III regime for banks and the US-Dodd Frank rules.

Recently, corporate criminal liability has taken a central spot in the international agenda. The G20 established that,

> There are several rationales for ensuring liability of corporations and other legal entities: today's economy, both at the national and international level, is mainly driven by commercial entities, i.e. legal persons. Fighting corruption would fall short if only the natural persons involved were punished while the legal person was exempt from sanctions [...] Ensuring that a legal person, as well as the culpable individuals, can be held liable can therefore have an important deterrent effect, motivating and incentivizing enterprises to make compliance a priority along with investing in adequate and effective internal controls, ethics and *compliance programmes* or measures to prevent and detect corruption.
>
> G20, 2017, p. 2, emphasis added

In the United Kingdom, the debate on Corporate Criminal Liability (CCL) has raised once again after the tragic events of the Grenfell Tower fire on 14 June 2017. Almost two months later, the metropolitan police gave the victims an update on the case saying they had reasonable grounds to suspect the Royal Borough of Kensington and Chelsea and the Kensington and Chelsea Tenant Management Organisation "may have committed the offence of Corporate Manslaughter and Corporate Homicide Act 2007" (Dodd & Sherwood, 2017). However, victims highlighted that the act foresees a punishment of unlimited fine (Section 1.6), and that no individual can be held liable for neither corporate manslaughter nor corporate homicide (Section 18). In this case, the victims did not perceive the potential punishment as proportionate or sufficient. In words of Yvette Williams, from Justice 4 Grenfell: "what we would like to see running alongside that is individuals being prosecuted. We want is individuals named and prosecuted—you can have both, but we don't want corporate manslaughter on its own" (BBC News, UK, 2017). This case along many others in the field of corporate risk management (Grimshaw vs. Ford; The Challenger Launch; the Perrier recall; etc.), sets out the question of whether a properly implemented CMS would be able (and have been able) to prevent those deaths.

While similar researches have been performed in the pharmaceutical field (Di Ronco, 2014) and regarding Italian football clubs (Lavorgna & Di Ronco, 2015), this work will build upon them and try to analyse some of the causes that might underlie the ineffectiveness/effectiveness of CMSs as instruments of deterrence. However, the present work will still concentrate on Corporations as objects of study. It will regard them as individuals and analyse their interaction in a determined socio-legal environment.

2 Literature Review

2.1 *Criminological Literature on Corporate Criminality*

2.1.1 White-collar Criminality

In 1933 the Michael-Adler Report pointed out the futility of the criminological research in those days (Laub, 2006, p. 237). Through a survey, they concluded that "criminological research has not yet achieved a single definite conclusion and (...) its utter lack of significance is due to defects in the planning or the execution of the researches" (Michael & Adler, 1933, p. 105, cited in Goff & Geis, 2008, p. 351). Following the report, criminology scholars focused on developing a science of behaviour. There was a need for a single explanation of criminal behaviours, not only crimes committed by the lower classes but also the bourgeois (Sutherland, 1940, p. 10).

In that sense, Sutherland's main thesis stroke the methodology implemented by traditional criminologists. One of the scholars that inspired Sutherland was Willem Adriaan Bonger (1969) (Braithwaite, 1985, p. 2; Friedrichs, 2017). Embedded in the Marxist branch of criminology, Bonger attributed the cause of deviance to the pressure suffered by the working class in capitalist societies. He also pointed out that a similar attitude rose from the bourgeois sector in times of capitalist prosperity. However, one of the main obstacles faced by his theory was the fact that it was not able to explain the high correlation between the variables of poverty and high criminality rates (Braithwaite, 1985, p. 2).

Sutherland casted doubt on that statistical correlation by pointing the biased nature of its data. The author highlighted that although official measures claimed the high incidence of crime in lower classes those measures referred "to criminals handled by the police, the criminal and juvenile courts, and the prisons, and to such crimes as murder, assault, burglary, robbery, larcency, sex offenses, and drunkenness" (Sutherland, 1940, p. 1). In that way, criminologist relied solely on data taken from agencies of the criminal justice vis-à-vis specific types of crimes. Thus, the lack of objectivity was not only found in the selectiveness of the police agency (Zaffaroni, 2013, p. 16), but in the reluctance of justice to criminalise business persons (Sutherland, 1944, p. 137). Sutherland pointed out two main causes of such bias: the resources inequality that enables a business man to scape criminal justice compared with the lower-class criminal; and that crimes committed by business persons fall under the administrative, civil or equity jurisdiction rather than the stigmatizing criminal justice (Sutherland, 1983, p. 6). The sample used by traditional criminologist was biased and thus inappropriate to give a representative picture of the population (Sutherland, 1940, p. 2; Agresti & Finlay, 1997).

To give a holistic explanation of crime, Sutherland called the attention to another sort of offence: white-collar crimes. In that way, this category was defined as “a crime committed by a person of respectability and high social status in the course of his occupation” (Sutherland, 1983, p. 7). By using the term “white collar” the author referred to business managers and executives, as it was used by Alfred P. Sloan in his book “An Autobiography of a White-Collar Worker” (Sutherland, 1983, p. 265). In other words, Sutherland included in his analysis of criminal populations a wide range of individuals with different social backgrounds and cultural features. This inclusion enabled scholars to search among a broader array of variables for those common denominators which may cause criminal behaviours.

Taking that into consideration, Sutherland adventured an explanation that could better fit both white-collar and common crimes. He divided his hypothesis in two sides of the same coin: the individual and the social. Regarding the first one, he explained that from the available data a possible elucidation was the differential association as a learning process. As he defined it,

> differential association is that criminal behavior is learned in association with those who define such criminal behavior favorably and in isolation from those who define it unfavorably, and that a person in an appropriate situation engages in such criminal behavior if, and only if, the weight of the favourable definitions exceeds the weight of the unfavorable definitions.
>
> SUTHERLAND, 1983, p. 240

On the other hand, the social side discusses the criminal behaviour from the viewpoint of society. It intrinsically refers to the process of initiation into crime (Sutherland, 1983, p. 255). This explanation is the concept of “social disorganization” which,

> May be either of two types: anomie, or the lack of standards which direct the behavior of members of a society in general or in specific areas of behavior; or the organization within a society of groups which are in conflict with reference to specific practices. Briefly stated, social disorganization may appear in the form of lack of standards or conflict of standards.
>
> SUTHERLAND, 1983, p. 255

In this way, the cultural element in Sutherland can be seen through his theory on differential association and social disorganisation (Sutherland, 1940, p. 11; on social disorganisation more recently revived by Bursik, 1988). As it will be explained in chapter 2.3, this cultural element refers to the context that facilitates the replication of criminal behaviours. This context might mean the individual learning process of criminal conducts within the subculture or the structural configuration that serves as fertile ground for criminal proliferation.

Furthermore, to depict the attitude of the so called "robber barons", Sutherland (1940, p. 2) quoted the question asked by Colonel Vanderbil: "You don't suppose you can run a railroad in accordance with the statutes, do you?" This question illustrates the disconnection between the "rules of the game" and the rule of law. Moreover, it insinuates that both business mores and formal laws are irreconcilable (Tombs & Whyte, 2015, p. 128). Still, this business/law dilemma may not explain entirely the corporate criminality.

Building upon differential association and social disorganisation, Ronald Aker developed the social-learning theory (Akers, 1998). The goal of this theory was to link Sutherland's work with general principles of behavioural psychology (Akers & Jennings, 2016, p. 230). The stress was put on personal interaction as the context in which social learning occurs. This theory divided the process of learning that can lead to deviant behaviours in two means: instrumental and vicarious. Regarding the first, the learning process happens directly through punishment or reward. On the contrary, vicarious learning process occurs through observation or imitation of a behaviour after the perception of its consequence (Krohn, 1999, p. 464). Moreover, Aker (1998, p. 323), acknowledges certain variables within a social structure that correlate with the outcome of any given social learning process.

Following this reasoning, the relevance of structures in the analysis of corporate criminality can be seen through the criminological Strain Theories (Young, 1981, p. 234; Donegan & Ganon, 2008, p. 4). According to these theories, the criminal behaviours have their roots in the conflict between culture and structure. In this sense, the individual aspirations are determined through cultural means, but they do not always correlate with the opportunities determined by the structure (Young, 1981, p. 237). That disconnection produces the strain which determines the criminal behaviour. This tension is commonly bore by group of individuals who experience the lack of means as a subculture. Thus, the subculture response would be a collective solution to the collective problem (Young, 1981, p. 237). In other words, social positions with culturally induced goals placed upon them will turn to illegitimate means to fulfil those goals (Becker, 1963, p. 26). In words of Robert K. Merton (1938, p. 679),

> The cultural demands made on persons in this situation are incompatible. On the one hand, they are asked to orient their conduct toward the prospect of accumulating wealth and on the other, they are largely denied effective opportunities to do so institutionally.

Is this lack of coordination between legitimate means and cultural goals that leads to anomie (Merton, 1938, p. 682). In this case, the social disorganisation appears in the form of conflict of standards. While the culture desire strives for its objective, it correlates with an illegitimate mean; or the lack of means skews the behaviour towards criminality. A classic example that represent this strain would be the "American Dream" and the social structure (Epstein, 2010, p. 72).

In the same way, Merton's idea of social dysfunction can be compared to the concept of social disorganisation of Sutherland for they both attempt a holistic explanation for criminal behaviour. As Merton defines it, social dysfunction is "a designated set of consequences of a designated pattern of behavior, belief, or organization that interfere with a designated functional requirement of a designated social system" (Merton & Nisbet, 1976, p. 732, cited in Segre, 2014, p. 212). These two theories can be categorised as functional analysis of social structures. Their observations attempt to deconstruct the process by which an environment fosters criminal behaviour in opposition to the legitimate expectation of the culture that encompass the subculture.

2.1.2 General Strain Theory

This theory connects with corporate criminality in a multilevel dimension, both in a macro and micro level of analysis (Britt & Rocque, 2016, p. 195). Thus, by including a wider range of variables into its potential explanations of strains, the General Strain Theory (GST) has better elements to explain corporate criminality (Langton & Piquero, 2007).

The GST was developed by Robert Agnew (1992). He pointed out the distinction between the strain theories, social control and differential association and social learning theories. In his terms, while the former stressed the negative relation with others, the social control focused on the absence of relationships with the conventional surroundings of an individual such as schools, family, friends, work, etc. Vis-à-vis the latter, its emphasis remains in the positive relation with other criminals. For that reason, Agnew asserts that the strain theory complements the other two theories, "and while these other theories view delinquency as the result of drift or of desire, strain theory views it as the result of pressure" (Agnew, 1992, p. 50).

In this way, Agnew's reformulation of the Strain Theory expanded the boundaries of the disconnection between cultural/subcultural expectations and the legitimate achievements towards fair/unfair outcomes. Rather than focusing on the unfeasibility of achieving certain positive goals, the GST concentrates on other sources of stress that can be stronger predictors of aggression or criminal behaviours. In this sense, he included all sorts of negative relations that could eventually contribute to the pressure (Agnew, 1992, p. 57–74; Huck, et al., 2017, pp. 1009–1010; Langton & Piquero, 2007, p. 2). Thus, the GST provides a broader vision of variables that can contribute to the pressure and eventually the strain that leads to a criminal behaviour. The resignification of the traditional Strain Theory offers a source of variables that could better contribute to explanation white-collar criminality as well as ordinary criminality (Langton & Piquero, 2007, p. 11; Agnew, 2016).

The ideologist of the GST also points out that while objective strains refer to "events or conditions that are disliked by most members of a given group" (Agnew, 2001, p. 320), subjective strains indicate "events or conditions that are disliked by the people who are experiencing (or have experienced) them" (Agnew, 2001, p. 321). Thus, considering the macro and micro level of the strains, it is the objective sources of strain that might result in the subjective strain. The individuals suffering this tension would tend to implement behavioural coping strategies to scape or reduce the suffer (Agnew, 2001, p. 326).

Additionally, these strains can be categorised in three main types: goal blockage, loss of positive stimuli, and the presentation on negative stimuli (Agnew, 2012, pp. 34–35). Regarding the first one, and in contrast with the traditional Strain Theory, the unachieved goals in the GST may include from the desire for more money in short periods of time to masculine status or high levels of autonomy, among others (Agnew, 2012, pp. 34–35). Likewise, the second type of strains can include from loss of money or property to family or partner issues (Agnew, 2012, p. 35). Lastly, the third type of strain relates to negative stimuli in the form of suffering criminal behaviours such as physical or physiological abuse (Agnew, 2012, p. 35). Moreover, there are some factors that have a stronger power of attraction towards criminal behaviours for they affect the ability to cope with the strain through a non-criminal mean (Agnew, 2001, p. 326). According to stress, justice and emotions literature (Agnew, 2001, p. 327), the strains would be more likely to result in criminal behaviours "when they (1) are seen as unjust, (2) are seen as high in magnitude, (3) are associated with low social control, and (4) creates some pressure or incentive to engage in criminal coping" (Agnew, 2001, p. 326).

To sum up, according to the GST, there are an array of strains (more than the ones considered by the traditional Strain Theory) that may lead to negative emotions creating pressure that may push individuals to crime (Agnew, 2016, p. 209).

2.1.3 Corporate Connection

While these theories where not originally developed to explain exclusively white-collar crimes or corporate crimes (Agnew, 2012; Young, 1981, p. 236), the connection between these crime typologies and the criminological theories developed in chapters 2.1 and 2.2 can be stablished through their composing elements. Accordingly, Langton and Piquero (2007, pp. 11–13) conclude that the GST might present a sufficiently broad explanation to be able to account for ordinary criminality and white-collar crime.

In this sense, while Sutherland still talked about white collar criminal as an individual, it leads the way to inquire the role of the corporations in crime, and thus search into corporate crimes. Moreover, authors such as Said, et al. (2014, p. 4), do not include in their definition of corporate crime the distinction between individuals committing a crime for the company and individuals committing a crime in the company for themselves. Although a wider definition might be helpful, further criminological work distinguished between offenses committed by members of the corporation for the corporation, offences committed by the corporation (Clinard & Quinney, 1973, p. 188) and occupational crimes, with the corporation as mean or trigger. Regarding the latter, its classification refers to individuals committing a crime for self-profit or against their employee during the curse of their occupations (Clinard & Quinney, 1973; Braithwaite, 1985, p. 19). Thus, the classification can be stated as occupational crime in opposition to corporate crime.

On the other hand, and from the legal point of view, if firms are legally constructed persons it can be argued their personal participation in occupational offences by providing the elements or the ground for it to happen. This debate may possibly circle around the charges filed against the companies, as secondary participants, or accomplices. However, as it will be developed in the next chapter, companies can also be the ones generating the criminal state of mind in the white-collar criminal's head. In such case, the offense would fall under the classification of corporate crime.

In this sense, we can think of the corporation as a micro society. Corporations appear as a controlled social environment that contain and institutionalise subcultures. They represent a laboratory study of micro behaviours susceptible of analysis and replication in a macro level through social control techniques (Gottfredson & Hirschi, 1990; Hagan, et al., 1985; Hirschi, 1977; Tittle, 1995; Kubrin & Wo, 2016; Hoffmann, 2003, pp. 755–756). In this sense, the macro-level control theories analyse the social disorganisation as a source of criminal deviance (Britt & Rocque, 2016, pp. 188–189). The aim of predicting or explaining individual behaviours in a multi subcultural context laid the query of how can organisations or subgroups auto-regulate or self-govern to minimise the risk of fostering deviant behaviours.

Here, far from the notion of state-corporate crime as a collusion between states and corporations (Michalowski & Kramer, 2006, p. 15; Said, et al., 2014, pp. 4–5), the corporation is presented as a state for the features it gathers. The corporation is presented as a vessel of multicultural subgroups with norms, symbols (such as the brand logo), values and goals. The analogy of organisations as societies within a society can also be transplanted to nation-states in the global context. Societies within the international community.

Supporting this connection, Donegan and Ganon (2008, pp. 5–6) point out that,

> Entities that have become large enough to acquire a bureaucratic social structure, whether major accounting firms or businesses, may contribute to macro-level strain if they adopt formal policies which make conventionally envisioned success unattainable for many of their employees. The up-or-out promotion policies practiced by major audit firms and Enron's "rank and yank" evaluations exemplify macro-level strain, as did the latter firm's display of current stock price throughout its headquarters […]. Persistent harassment by supervisors, which can include impossible demands for productivity, is a fertile source of micro-level strain. Excessive overtime is a macro-level factor when caused by market competition, but may be viewed as micro-level when used by a hostile supervisor to intimidate or punish subordinates. Since GST focuses on the socio-psychological aspects of the causes of strain, which includes individual workers' status in their firms, it can be successfully integrated with cultural deviance theories focusing on corporate culture.

Considering the definition provided by Elliott Jaques (1951, p. 251) the organisational culture can be seen as a,

> […] customary and traditional way of thinking and doing things, which is shared to a greater or lesser degree by all members, and which the new members must learn and at least partially accept, in order to be accepted into the services of the firm.

Kilmann et al. (1985, cited in Martin, 1998, p. 330) added to this definition the idea that organisational culture is a reflection of common values, beliefs, assumptions, attitudes, expectations and norms. According to this view, the organisational culture is something that develops over time and not something that can be created out of thin air. Specific terminology or the use of slang comparable to drug or military culture evidence the existence of subcultures within a firm or the subculture of the whole firm (Donegan & Ganon, 2008, pp. 16–17). Cases such as Siemens (Klinkhammer, 2013), Enron (Cohan, 2002; Markoff, 2012), Qwest, BMS and MicroStrategy (Donegan & Ganon, 2008) revealed in that sense, similar patterns of subcultural features.

Following this logic, it is worth considering that the deviant behaviour may not be regarded as such within the boundaries of the group that serves as environment for the social learning. The objective strain ontologically suffered by the subgroup become a part of it, a problem that is handle to the individual as soon as he or she becomes a member, and influences the perception of such strain. In other words, the subgroup that propagates its own subculture and sub-norms, may not consider its practice as deviant for they become a part of their group identity or cultural consciousness (Sanchez & Vargas, 2016, p. 161). As it is discussed by Stein (2013, p. 792), people tend to create own intentions to conform the majority even if they know the majority is wrong. This bias may proof to be an obstacle when arguing the mental element in corporate crimes.

Nevertheless, without falling into the relativism of stating that a deviant behaviour will be so depending on the perspective of the person who judges, the social creation of the subgroup and the subjection to the State's control diminishes the subcultural perspective. The persons that integrate the subgroup are still bound to obey the law of the society they live in, on a macro level. In this sense, the firm is categorised as a citizen embedded in a national culture. Thus, rather than a convergence perspective with a predominant culture of the organisation, the deontological legal approach would be divergence with an organisational adaptation to the local culture (Martin, 1998, p. 345; Lammers & Hickson, 1979). In other words, while the convergence perspective states that the national culture is servile to organisations, the divergence perspective supports the rule of the national culture over the organisation. Contrary to the sophoclean moral dilemma in *Antigona*, the law of society ought to prevail. However, as it will be developed later in this work, the feasibility of this compliance may not be as straightforward as a plain legal imposition.

As it was seen through this chapter, the analysis of macro-level linkages for deviant behaviours has been a consistent topic in criminology (Hoffmann,

2003). The reviewed literature leaves the enigma of how can corporations reduce the impact of all the possible strains that may lead to criminal behaviours.

2.2 *Corporate Engagement in Social Interaction*

2.2.1 Organisational Behaviour

At this point the literature on Organisational Behaviour (Martin, 1998; McFarland & Gómez, 2014; Knights & Willmott, 2011), Corporate Governance and Signaling Theory (Spence, 1973; Karasek & Bryant, 2012) needs to be mention. Furthermore, these topics have a close connection with the criminological theories developed in chapters 2.1 and 2.2. Their relation can be explained through the object of study that each theory addresses. Although through different means and basis, they all relate to the study of individuals and their interaction with a group. Thus, they can also be connected to corporations, for they are commonly implemented to manage processes and results within the firm (Martin, 1998, pp. 25–26).

That been said, as it was pointed out by Thomas Schelling (2006, p. 141), "the hearts and minds and motives and habits of millions of people who participate in a segregated society may or may not bear close correspondence with the massive results that collectively they can generate". These words put forward the idea that macro behaviours or organisational outcomes may not be explained or anticipated by focusing on individual desires. Moreover, the individual states of mind might be completely contrary to the aggregated result. Schelling also refers to how individuals interact in a communication system. Everything that a person does or implies sends information to the network and by that they exercise de network (Schelling, 2006, p. 40). Likewise, it can even be counterproductive for the interest of the individual if every other member of the group makes the same choice (Schelling, 2006, p. 209). This decision theory-based paradox, as a progression of the game theory, reflects the complex situation of decision-making in a context in which several actors interact under many rational elements while seeking a goal (Enicov, 2016, p. 284). In this sense, organisations become ideal sites to grasp how the individual motives and goals interact with each other, albeit at the same time trying to fulfil the purpose of the gestalt.

For that reason, firms implement organisational behaviour (OB) studies as managerial tools to analyse and plan desired outcomes. OB can be defined as "a field of study that investigates the impact individuals, groups and structure have on behavior within organizations, for the purpose of applying that knowledge toward improving an organization's effectiveness." (Robbins & Judge, 2014, p. 28). Opposite to the study of social interaction in the quest for the origins of criminal behaviours, OB aims to analyse the social phenomenon to enhance the effectiveness of the firm. Effectiveness that strives for economical profit. The study of the organisation then becomes a multidisciplinary task nurtured by sociology, psychology, economics, politics, anthropology, etc. (Robbins & Judge, 2014, pp. 29–30; Brewis, et al., 2017, p. 7), all applied to achieve the same profitable goal.

2.2.2 Corporate Governance

Following this reasoning, corporate governance (CG) "denotes the rules of business decision-making and directs the internal mechanism of companies for following those rules. It includes the customs, policies, laws and institutions that impact the way a corporation is directed, administered or controlled" (Rahim & Alam, 2014, p. 607). Additionally, the authors mention that because of several corporate scandals the concept has recently included ethic codes, accountability, disclosure, etc. (also Sir Adrian Cadbury, 2000, cited in Eijsbouts, 2017, p. 187). In other words, the results obtained through OB become the design implemented through CG.

In that sense, Angel Gurría, OECD Secretary-General, asserts that "the purpose of corporate governance is to help build an environment of trust, transparency and accountability necessary for fostering long-term investment, financial stability and business integrity, thereby supporting stronger growth and more inclusive societies." (OECD, 2015, p. 7). This definition divides the objectives of CG into benefits for the company and for society as a whole. However, the definition gives us a glimpse on the economical perspective of business towards society. By using the connector "thereby", the definition assumes that supporting growth and inclusive societies is also a factor that helps foster long-term investments and business profit. Thus, the corporate conceptualisation of social responsibility may be seen as strongly related to profit. A way of reassuring long-term good business.

2.2.3 Corporate Social Responsibility

Regarding Corporate Social Responsibility (CSR), authors like Heugens and Oosterhout point out that its conceptualisation lacks clarity. They assert that its causes and consequences are unclear, thus its implementation becomes unhelpful and so the concept should be dispensed (Heugens & Oosterhout, 2008, p. 198). On the other hand, authors like Brewis et al. define CSR as the "practices and policies undertaken by organizations to promote the idea that they have concerns that extend beyond efficiency, performance, productivity and profit to embrace the public, customers, the environment and other stakeholders" (Brewis, et al., 2017, p. 565).

The traditional conception of CSR interpreted that the only responsibility corporations had was profit (Friedman, 1970). However, Friedman named the CSR as a "fundamentally subversive doctrine" which gives us a glimpse on the post-war scenario in which his thesis took place. The adjective "subversive" shows the pro capitalist discourse from which the author articulated his arguments. Albeit this brief hermeneutic analysis (Sarantakos, 2013, p. 334–335) might be the root of his advocacy for attributing no further responsibility than the one stablished by the rule of law, it is worth mentioning the scope of its consequence. Accordingly, Friedman asserted that the only responsibility for corporations was to increase "its profit so long as it stays within the rules of the game, which is to say, engages in open and free competition without deception or fraud" (Friedman, 1970). This liberal perspective on CSR can be traced into the political/legal concept of CSR that this work proposes. Although devoid of political connotation, this work interprets CSR in a similar way as Friedman did.

In a more specific way, CSR can be related in this research with some features of Corporate Citizenship (CC) and Corporate Social Performance (CSP) as two of the four ideal types of CSR theories named by Melé (2009, pp. 48–49). Regarding the latter, Wood (1991, p. 693) defines it as "a business organization's configuration of principles of social responsibility, processes of social responsiveness, and policies, programs, and observable outcomes as they relate to the firm's societal relationships". Under this categorization authors like Keith Davis confront Friedman's free market ideas and assert that CSR begins where the law ends (Davis, 1973, p. 313). Moreover, he argues that the raison d'être of business institutions is to offer a social service. By referring to the Iron Law of Responsibility, the author related the greater power owned by corporations with their social impact and the duty to use it for social benefit or lose it (Davis, 1973, p. 314; Melé, 2009, p. 52). In a more moderate way, Wood understood the principle of public responsibility within CSP as the extension of corporate accountability for "outcomes related to their primary and secondary areas of involvement with society" (Wood, 1991, p. 697). In other words, corporations would not have to handle all social problems but they would have to deal with problems they have caused or that relate to their business operations and interests (Wood, 1991, p. 697). In that sense, business and society are seen as interwoven rather than distinct (Melé, 2009, p. 53). Regarding the individual responsibility Woods refer that managers should not avoid personal responsibility for not looking after socially responsible outcomes of corporate actions by shielding behind rules, policies or procedures (Wood, 1991, p. 699).

On the other hand, while CSP is grounded in sociology, CC is based on political studies. According to Melé (2009, p. 70), the conceptual bases of CC can be founded in the notion of "citizenship" used by Aristotle. This concept implies the existence of rights and obligations within the political community. Firms are ontologically individuals created by society thus they have the same duty of contributing to the common good of people (Solomon, 1992, p. 184, cited in Melé, 2009, p. 71). Moreover, this conceptualisation of CC is consistent with the definition of citizen. If we understand that a citizen is a "legally recognized subject or national of a nation or commonwealth" (Oxford Dictionaries, 2017), we identify the normative nature of the citizenship. Thus, there is no logical argument to exclude normatively constructed persons. Although it exceeds the scope of this work, it is worth mentioning that authors like Logsdon and Wood (2002, pp. 156–157) argue a transition from a local citizen conception towards a global business citizenship which reframes "the moral grounding of CSR within the language of citizenship" (Logsdon & Wood, 2002, p. 155).

The thesis of Friedman (1970) is specifically cited as the conceptual bases for the Shareholder Value Theory (SVT) of one of the four theories that aim to explain CSR according to Melé (2009, p. 58). Nevertheless, as ideal types may not be observed in reality as purely as they are conceived, the concept of CSR supported in this work can be described as eclectic. It takes several aspects of CC for it understands firms as socially constructed persons through the legal attribution of personhood. Regarding CSP, it also acknowledges the fact that because of the special power corporations have nowadays the legally requested duty of care ought to follow higher standards than the rest of individuals with less power. Moreover, the duty of care increases when the firm gets involved in especially risky situations or business. In this way, the eclectic proposition of this work does not contradict the SVT for it also recognises the duty to comply with the law. However, the governmental delineation of the "rules of the game" might not be the same as when Friedman developed his thesis (Friedman, 1962).

It was presented here two plausible interpretations of CSR. On the one hand, from the legal point of view, CSR can be seen as the corporate duty to obey the law and prevent harm to third parties. While on the other hand, the concept offered by the economic discipline includes the promotion of the idea that there is more to corporations than just profit. Moreover, the economical approach can be related with Zizek's concept of ethical consumption (The Pervert's Guide to Ideology, 2012, mins. 55:46 to 57:51). Zizek explained ethical consumption through the Starbucks case in which the company sells not only coffee but the idea that for each coffee that the customer buys he will be helping people in need. In that sense, CSR is transferred into the prices of the commodity and used as a marketing technique to increase gains. Therefore, the consumer and the firm fulfil their social/moral duties while enjoying the commodity and profit respectively. Thus, economical conceptualisations of both CG and CSR reaffirm the theory that CSR "is not something antithetical to profitability, but it is one of the strategic means by which profitability might be secured, protected, extended and maximised." (Tombs & Whyte, 2015, p. 122).

As it is also pointed out by other scholars, the concept of CSR is rather fluid, without precision nor consent among the academia (Rahim & Alam, 2014, p. 609). For that reason, it is necessary to highlight that this work will focus on CSR from the legal point of view, as a recognition of social responsibility (Tombs & Whyte, 2015, p. 117). In other words, CSR is understand as the corporate guarantee that it will abide by the laws that regulate their life and activity just like the rest of individuals within any given society.

Authors like Tombs and Whyte (2015, pp. 108–128) argue that the new form of shareholding corporation segregate the ownership from the control or management. Thus, there is a cleavage between the interest of the shareholders and the senior managers. Consequently, the real owners resign their control over the firm and directors benefit from their monthly payment rather than the welfare of the corporation. That division has not only an impact on the work process but also on the legal responsibilities that lay upon shareholders and managers. By resigning the control over the organisation, owners may use the legal personhood of the corporation to shield them from the law. Moreover, the delegation of responsibilities can trigger thorough debates regarding legal terms such as knowledge and duty of care. While arguing this, the authors state that there is nothing in the DNA of the corporations that makes them prioritise the wellbeing of society over the interest of the firm (Tombs & Whyte, 2015, p. 128). Therefore, they assert that the inclusion of corporate social responsibilities in CG proves a conflict of interest for managers that now must ensure corporate profit maximisation and social welfare. Two tasks that may not always be susceptible of simultaneous achievement.

2.2.4 Signaling Theory

Lastly, the signaling theory was developed by Spence (1973) through the analysis of the job market. He stressed that the decision of an employer to hire a person is comparable with the lottery. The author puts forward the idea that when an employer hires someone, he is betting on the benefits that the person will bring to his company for he might learn about the real capabilities of the individual afterwards. In this sense, the employee candidate presents himself to the employer through signals and indices. The latter consists in attributes of the person unrelated with the image he presents for the job. On the other hand, signals are defined as "observable characteristics attached to the individual that are subject to manipulation by him" (Spence, 1973, p. 357), such as education. Therefore, signaling theory stablishes that confronted with uncertain decisions parties exchange signals to reduce the information asymmetry, and thus the intrinsic risk of the choice (Colwell, et al., 2011, p. 48; Certo, 2003, p. 434; Rindova, et al., 2006, p. 54). In this way, "signaling theory is useful for theorizing how decision makers with incomplete information make decisions of an interdependent nature, such as when buyers make decisions regarding their choice of supplier" (Colwell, et al., 2011, p. 48).

In this way, the signalling theory relates to CG and CSR in a similar way through market logics. Their formal and thorough implementation in companies can be interpreted as a signal for further business opportunities. This utility of CSR supports the theory that understands it as a corporate strategy rather than an expression of genuine concern for society (Tombs & Whyte, 2015, p. 128).

However, this signal can have two consequences. On the one hand, the firm might invest in a serious process of CG with a genuine concern for CSR, in which case according to the signalling theory, buyers and suppliers may perceive the organisation as an ethical company. This can lead to them considering the reputational benefits and risk reduction of engaging in business with an ethical company, and therefore accepting the commercial transaction. In this way, the ethical signal as a better chance for business opportunity reflects in the profits of the signalling firm (Colwell, et al., 2011, p. 49). On the other hand, the CSR mechanism can also be implemented to give an appearance of ethicality. This last hypothetical case was presented by Trevino and Weaver (2001, p. 667) as "window dressing" (also see Friedman, 1970). These authors pointed out the importance of organisational context and timing when launching an ethical programme. They stablished that,

> The recent history of an organization may frame employees' perceptions of the purpose of any ethics initiative. For example, if an ethics initiative is adopted in the midst of a publicized scandal involving high level executives, the ethics initiative may be interpreted by employees as a transitory "window dressing" response to that scandal, and thus something that employees may ignore, even if the initiative had nothing to do with that scandal.
>
> TREVINO & WEAVER, 2001, p. 667

In this sense, the context in which ethical features of CG address CSR can also be seen as signals by buyers and suppliers. Moreover, these authors found a significant correlation between the fairness in the treatment employees receive from the firm and of organisational justice and the success of ethical programmes (Trevino & Weaver, 2001, p. 668). They conclude that the perception of organisational justice may proof an explanatory variable of ethical or unethical behaviours, as well as the support of employees to the ethical programme.

As it will be developed in chapter 2.4, the "window dressing" can affect both the signaling effect towards business opportunities and the legal solution to the imposition of genuine CSR process.

Along this chapter there were presented the studies on OB, CG and Signaling Theory. This added an economical perspective on corporate crime in contrast with the criminological theories which search for the explanatory variable of corporate criminal behaviours. The notions of CG and CSR showed the main tools that cross the three disciplines, and how they interact on economical and legal levels. The understanding of this dynamic in a complex context of individuals, organisations, markets, and governments sheds light on the reasons for social equilibriums. Nonetheless, as Schelling (2006, pp. 26–27) affirmed, an equilibrium analysis does not always mean an expression of approval but instead, it is merely a description of a state. Thus, this chapter analysed the tools that could have contributed to the processes of adjustment that might have led to a certain equilibrium between corporate development and social tolerability of harm. This equilibrium may be deduced from the explanations of criminal deviance in corporate contexts or through the organisational procedures and variables that contribute to either criminal behaviour or genuine CSR. Following this analysis, the next chapter will present the deontological perspective of law in order to delineate the "rules of the game".

2.3 *Compliance Management Systems*

As it will be described in this chapter, Compliance Management Systems (CMSs) can be categorised under CG as a scheme implemented to foster a culture of compliance with the law within an organisation. Furthermore, this compliance culture has close implications regarding CSR, corporate ethics, and legal charges.

In that sense, the Federal Deposit Insurance Corporation (FDIC) from the U.S.A. government defines a CMS as a way in which institutions face their responsibilities. Is the way in which organisations learn about their compliance responsibilities; guarantees the understanding of those responsibilities across all its members; introduce the requirements into its processes; reviews operations and ensures that the responsibilities are met; and, based on the review, corrects and updates the system as needed (Federal Deposit Insurance Corporation, 2017, pp. II-3.1). Moreover, the FDIC identifies two components of the CMS: Compliance Program (CP) and the Board and Management oversight (Federal Deposit Insurance Corporation, 2017, pp. II-3.1).

On the other hand, as it was mentioned in the introduction, the ISO 19600 defines Management Systems as a "*set of interrelated or interacting elements of an organization to establish policies and objectives and processes to achieve those objectives*" (International Organization for Standardization, 2014, pp. 2–3). The ISO also points out that a properly implemented CMS enables the organisation to show a serious commitment to obey the law, may that be hard law, soft law, or technical good practices. Additionally, CMS allow corporations to prove "good corporate governance, best practices, ethics, and community expectations" (International Organization for Standardization, 2014, p. v).

Furthermore, CMSs were referred by the Basel Committee on Banking Supervision (BCBS) (2005, p. 14) in relation to the compliance function, emphasising that it

> Should be carried out under a compliance programme that sets out its planned activities, such as the implementation and review of specific policies and procedures, compliance risk assessment, compliance testing, and educating staff on compliance matters. The compliance programme should be risk-based and subject to oversight by the head of compliance to ensure appropriate coverage across businesses and co-ordination among risk management functions.

Concordantly, Ulrich Beck (1992, p. 21) understood risk in methodological terms. In this way, he defined it as "systematic way of dealing with hazards and insecurities induced and introduced by modernization itself". Thus, the author depicted risk through its connection with hazard and the way it was perceived now and before. While in the middle ages the danger might have resulted from the low supply of hygienic technology, nowadays it is a product of industrial overproduction which increases with globalisation (Beck, 1992, p. 21).

Considering this conceptualisation of risk, the BCBS restricted the concern towards risk to the hazards associated with the business activities of the bank (Basel Committee on Banking Supervision, 2005, p. 14). Thus, the CMS would be based and limited to the risks that concern the business activity. The same can be said about the scope of CMS according to the ISO 19600 (2014, p. 4.3). In this sense, the restriction of the application extent can be associated with the CSP theory of CSR (Wood, 1991, p. 697).

As the flowchart in figure 1 shows, CMSs consist on a complex structure with two main phases: establishment and improvement. During the first phase, there is an initial assessment of internal and external issues as well as

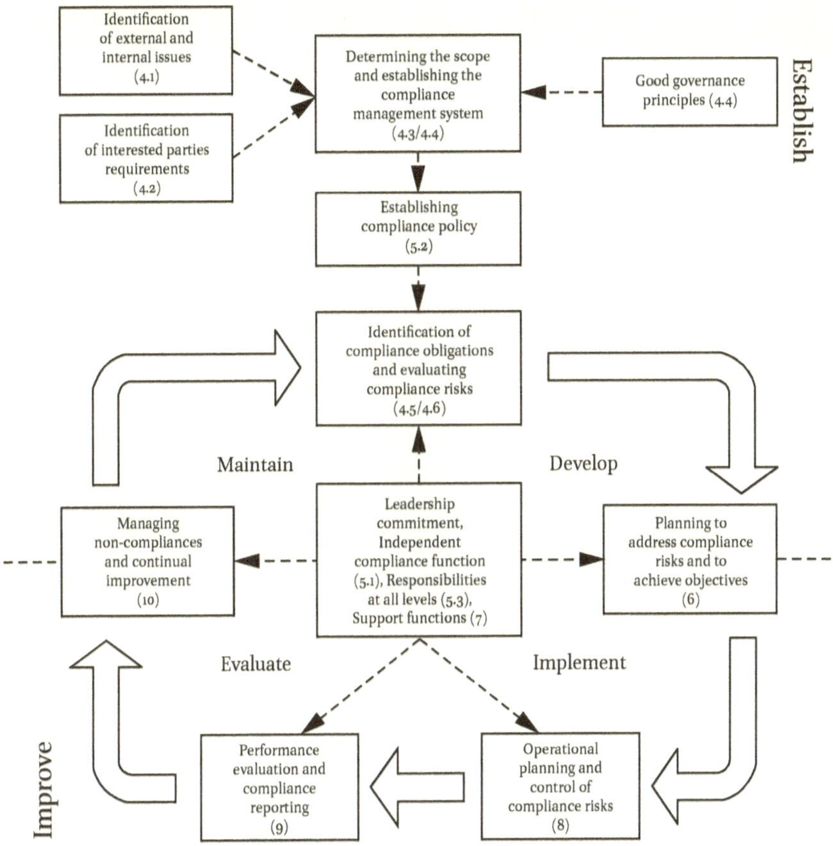

FIGURE 1 Flowchart of a Compliance Management System (International Organization for Standardization, 2014, p. vi)

obligations and requirements which the company ought to meet. At this stage good governance principles are mentioned as an element that must be present through all the design. In this sense, there are mentioned: the complete independence of the compliance officer; his direct access to the governing body; and an adequate provision of resources and authority (International Organization for Standardization, 2014, p. 4.4). Also at this instance is where the code of conduct or ethics code is developed. This code should reflect the core values of the firm as well as the commitment to legal requirements (International Organization for Standardization, 2014, p. 5.1). As it can also be seen in the flowchart, at its centre lays the leadership commitment, independence of compliance officer, distribution of responsibilities and support. These elements jointly with the compliance training of the organisation members are implemented to develop a compliance culture within the firm (International

Organization for Standardization, 2014, p. 7.3.2.3). Finally, the improvement phase is where the evaluation and control of risk takes place. Also, during this stage is when the implementation of a hotline and whistle-blowing systems take place (International Organization for Standardization, 2014, p. 5.3.4.f).

In this sense, CMS can be categorised as a specie of CG while it is also driven by its principles. Compliance Management Systems would be a way of Corporate Governance that concentrates in the requirements that a corporation need to meet, may them be legal or not. They became an internal tool of self-regulation as well as a source of external legitimacy (Eijsbouts, 2017, pp. 182–183). Additionally, the system has several elements that helps it build the ethical culture of compliance. Thus, relevant instruments are the code of conduct or ethics code, the hotlines for complains, whistle-blowing systems, compliance training, etc. Moreover, being that CMSs are risk based, they are designed to manage the hazards that a company might encounter in its activity. These dangers can include from punishment for offences such as bribery or fraud to a civil breach of contract. As it will be developed in the next chapter, CMSs may also play a relevant role when justifying corporate punishment and corporate criminal liability.

2.4 *Corporate Criminal Law*

> The white collar crime literature does have important implications for jurisprudence. Three elements of the literature come together to establish this relevance. The first of these is the literature demonstrating the massive numbers of unpunished white collar offenders in the community and the enormous damage to persons and property caused by their offending (...). Second is the literature arguing that protection of the public from white collar crime is better achieved by compliance law enforcement systems than by deterrence law enforcement systems. The third is the literature showing that ordinary citizens have had remarkably punitive attitudes recently toward white collar crime.
>
> BRAITHWAITE, 1985, p. 13

The legal problems that rise with corporate criminality are not new to literature nor jurisprudence. In this sense, the corporate crimes stretch the theory of crime and raise questions in the core of the judicial foundation (Silva Sanchez, 2016, pp. 7–10). Two of the principal questions that can be spot vis-à-vis corporate criminality are the definition of act as a human behaviour and the causality that connects the act with the result (Fletcher, 2000, p. 359; Silva Sanchez, 2016, p. 7). Moreover, regarding the culpability as a reproach for the criminal wrong, the traditional conception of criminal law was conceived addressing moral agents. Furthermore traditional criminal law considered cases such as homicide that are *malum in se*. For that reason, corporate criminality presents a cohesion challenge for criminal liability and legal theory of crime.

2.4.1 Action and Causality

As it was pointed out by Fletcher (2000, p. 358), these problems can be tracked back to the Bible (Exodus 21:28–29) as it was necessary that the action had an immediate relation with the result. The case the contractor that anticipates three deaths in his dangerous project (Fletcher, 2000, p. 363) is an example of causality issues. On the other hand, the case of a fly that gets into the eye of the driver which causes a reflex act that produces a deathly accident (Eser & Burkhardt, 1995, p. 69) is an examples of action issues.

Regarding the latter, although it might sound redundant, every punishable act should be first categorised as an action (Eser & Burkhardt, 1995, p. 72; Fletcher, 2000, p. 420). In this sense, the relevance of this concept for criminal law as well as the delimitation of the concept led to years of debate. The same happened with its antonym: omission (Fletcher, 2000, p. 421). However, what they both have in common is that they can be categorised as conducts (Fletcher, 2000, p. 421). In this way, the literature of actions debated several issues. An example would be the teleological theory which included the will in its concept, thus excluding involuntary acts such as reflex acts (Fletcher, 2000, p. 433; Zaffaroni, et al., 2002, p. 403). Nowadays, the personal theory of action developed by Roxin defines the action as the manifestation of the personality (Roxin, 1997, p. 252). Regardless of the theory followed and the nature of the debate, the consensus among scholars is that an action must be human. Moreover, authors like Roxin ascribe to the concept of action the purpose of excluding things that are exempt of criminal judgement, such as thoughts or acts of fictitious persons (Roxin, 1997, p. 234). Thus, the first problem that corporate criminality presents to the legal system is that companies are not susceptible of acting.

Regarding causality, scholars distinguished two levels of analysis: the ontological and the normative. On the ontological stage, the importance is to distinguish which action caused the result. This analysis takes place on a naturalistic/scientific sense (Roxin, 1997, p. 346). Therefore, the dominant theory at this level of analysis is the "but for" theory (Fletcher, 2000, p. 599) or theory of *condicio sine qua non* or equivalence of conditions (Roxin, 1997, p. 347). According to this theory, every action which without the result would not have happened would be a cause of the outcome. While the critics of this theory argue that it does not explain fortuity causations such as the single slap that ended in death because the victim had haemophilia (Fletcher, 2000, p. 600).

Answering to that criticism, Roxin highlights that this level of analysis is necessary but not sufficient to establish the criminal behaviour, for that it is required the normative level of analysis (Roxin, 1997, pp. 349–350).

In that sense, because of the modern risk societies we live in (Beck, 1992), the law stablishes certain levels of tolerable risk that people can undertake. On the other hand, the law also stablishes a duty of care to any individual that handles a dangerous thing or situation so as to minimise the chances of harm (see for example section 2 of the Corporate Manslaughter and Corporate Homicide Act 2007; article 142 of the Spanish Criminal Code; article 43 of the Italian Criminal Code; among others). Moreover, within the normative level of causality the conduct would be imputable to a person if his or her act went over the socially tolerable risk, and that risk was the one that materialised in the result (Roxin, 1997, pp. 365–385).

In this way, firms must deal with a double management of risks. On the one hand, the economic risk of daily business and on the other the risk that its activity produces to society. According to the latter, corporations ought to deal with their CSR in terms of preventing harm. Additionally, they must abide by the laws and regulations that stablish the tolerable risk. This due diligence is placed upon any individual, fictitious or real, to avoid the negligent state of mind as constitutive element of any offence, with the exception of strict liability (Fletcher, 2000, p. 716). When compulsory by law, CMSs represent a normative statement of tolerable risk. Thus, not implementing a CMS would imply an assumption of responsibility for the outcome of that taken risk.

Another normative analysis that becomes relevant for corporations derives from the sociological concept of illegality adopted by Niklas Luhmann. The author understood illegality as a "behaviour that violates formalized expectations" (Luhmann, 1964, cited in Klinkhammer, 2013, p. 194). In that sense, this definition of illegality splits the concept and expands the application towards not only legal norms. In other words, illegality would encompass any behaviour that went against what other members of the group expect from someone. Thus, while normatively illegal, an action can be useful to the goals of the organisation. According to Klinkhammer, this concept of useful illegality "provides sociology with a bridge to the criminological concept of corporate crime—by adding a focus on organizational norms" (Klinkhammer, 2013, p. 194).

This understanding of expectations was acknowledged in criminal law by Günther Jakobs. In that way, the author interpreted the normative analysis. In that sense, Jakobs defined the concept of roles as "a system of positions established in a normative way, occupied by interchangeable individuals; therefore, it is an institution based on people" (Jakobs, 1996, p. 22). The author distinguished two types of roles: the special and the common. Regarding the first, the special role develops as a product of someone needing to develop a common world or reality with other individuals. An example of it would be the role of a father or the assisting services in case of an emergency (Jakobs, 1996, p. 71). On the other hand, the common role refers to the role of respecting the law and respecting the rights of others in contrast with the individual rights (Jakobs, 1996, p. 72). In that sense, the field of legal enterprises presents a challenge in those cases in which the special role defined through an organisational norm contradicts the common role defined by the formal social norm. Therefore, the useful illegality theory may present a link between criminological theories, organisational theories, and legal solutions (Klinkhammer, 2013, pp. 195–196).

2.4.2 Liability

Another issue that rises within corporate criminal liability is the possibility to attribute culpability to corporations. If criminal liability implies moral blame, only moral subjects would be capable of understanding the consequence of their actions and thus freely choosing between behaving in accordance to law or against it (Wolf, 1985, cited in Gobert & Punch, 2003, p. 46). In this sense, the reasoning implemented by Wolf derives from what is called "atomic view" which places the responsibility of the corporate offence to the individual member whose act resulted in the crime. Following this logic, Wolf argued that sociopaths should also be exempted from criminal responsibility, for they were not capable of understanding the consequences of their actions. While Gobert and Punch (2003, p. 47) acknowledged this atomic view, they argued that it was ill-conceived and dangerous for it would release companies and sociopaths from the consequences of their harm (Gobert & Punch, 2003, pp. 48–49). However, contrary to Gobert and Punch awareness of the work developed by Wolf, she stated that

> Although organizations lack the capacity to be motivated to adopt moral goals and constraints, they have the capacity to be guided by them. Since they have this capacity, there seems no reason not to insist that they exercise it. That is, it is not unreasonable to hold organizations practically responsible, to insist that they act within moral constraints in the sense that they be liable for covering the costs and paying the consequences for the harmful and immoral action they perform.
>
> WOLF, 1985, p. 282

Nevertheless, the author concluded that as long as criminal law includes expressions of moral blame, it should not be applied directly to Corporations (Wolf, 1985, p. 286). In contrast with this view, Gobert and Punch present the "organic model". According to this view, the organisation is perceived as a gestalt, more closely related to the way people perceive companies. As it was presented by the authors, "when ordinary people refer to IBM, BT and Esso, for example, they do so without having in mind any particular individual or individuals" (Gobert & Punch, 2003, p. 49). In this sense, the authors present a casuistic solution to corporate liability by concluding that whether a company should be criminally liable will depend on the circumstances of the case. If the company endorsed or encouraged illegality, it would be reasonable to prosecute the company and not the worker (Gobert & Punch, 2003, p. 50).

In that sense, there are three main doctrines that dispute an explanation of corporate criminal liability: vicarious liability, identification doctrine, and autonomous liability or organisational fault. Regarding the first one, it refers to the liability of a person for the conduct of another under his responsibility. In the case of corporate criminality, the firm would be held responsible for the actions or omissions of its employee. This kind of liability does not require any proof of personal fault from the subject held liable (Ferguson, 1999, p. 164; Silva Sanchez, 2016, p. 297; Gobert & Punch, 2003, p. 55; Fletcher, 2000, p. 647). In this sense, this kind of liability can be related to complicity (Fletcher, 2000, p. 647), in the way it held responsible to the person that provided the environment for the offence to happen or did not prevent it. Moreover,

> the doctrine of vicarious liability imposed on companies a 'private policing' role, enlisting them in the prevention of crime by their employees, Presumably, if a company discovered that an employee was acting illegally, it would take corrective measures to remedy the situation in order to avoid its own prosecution. If the prosecution were to be limited to the individual at fault, the company would have no incentive to discourage the individual's actions, particularly if they were beneficial to the company.
>
> GOBERT & PUNCH, 2003, p. 56

Regarding the identification doctrine, it was developed in the English leading case *Tesco Supermarkets Ltd v Nattrass* (1971). According to this model of criminal liability,

> The acts and state of mind of certain senior officers in a corporation—the directing minds of the corporation—are deemed to be the acts and state of mind of the corporation. The directing minds are identified as the corporation. The corporation is considered (fictionally) to be *directly* liable, rather than *vicariously* liable.
>
> FERGUSON, 1999, p. 164

In that sense, a firm would be criminally liable only for the crimes committed by people who can be identified with the company (Gobert & Punch, 2003, p. 63). Thus, the English model of corporate liability established an *alter ego* embodied in certain employees. According to this doctrine, the employees can be divided into those who act as the hand of the firm and those who act as the mind of it (Wells, 1999, p. 120). The main difference with the vicarious liability model is that it instead of analysing the act of the individual as being on behalf of the company, it analyses it as it was the company itself. Therefore, within the identification doctrine not all employees can act as if they were the company, only senior members can represent the state of mind or *mens rea* of the firm (Ferguson, 1999, p. 164). In the case of vicarious liability it is not required a corporate *mens rea* (Ferguson, 1999, p. 165).

Finally, the organisational fault model differs from the other two typologies in the sense that it does not depend on showing a human error or misconduct (Gobert & Punch, 2003, p. 86). While on the other two doctrines the luck of the corporation depended on the individuals responsibility, in the organisational fault the corporation stands liable on its own (Wells, 2001, p. 157). The question in this doctrine is where to locate the fault of the corporation when holding a firm criminally liable of an unlawful conduct. Thus, "organisational fault inheres in a company's culpable failure to prevent business-related crimes that could have been adverted had a proper attention been paid to the risk of criminality" (Gobert & Punch, 2003, p. 86). In this sense, the negligence of the company would be found in their failure to prevent the negligence or illegality of its members. Through this doctrine, the liability lays on the lack of a risk based organised structure. A system that minimises the risk of criminal behaviours, hence embracing compliance (Wells, 2001, p. 155).

2.4.3 Why Criminal Law?

Because of the particular features that a corporate criminal law presents, which some have already been mentioned in this work (2.d.i; 2.d.ii), it can be deduced that corporate criminal law would require an unorthodox way of criminal law (Aller Maisonnave, 2016). As it was pointed out by Wells (2001, p. 14), on a broad sense criminal law has been debated between having a symbolic and a moral purpose. While the first one has a practical intention, the second represents a statement towards a categorical imperative of justice (Kant, 2012, pp. 33–34). These purposes are clearly related with the constitutive question in criminal law: Why does punishment exist? Accordingly, the main two theories of punishment argue between achieving a deterrent effect on criminal behaviours or a retributive purpose more related with the morality of punishment (Roxin, 1997, pp. 81–103; Wells, 2001, p. 18; Mir Puig, 2005, pp. 83–106).

In that sense, criminal law can be considered as a tool of social control, although not the only one possessed by the government (Mir Puig, 2005, p. 50). However, the *ultima ratio* characteristic of criminal law is given for the severity of the punishments it delivers. Thus, it is the ultima threat or resource a government must appeal to (Mir Puig, 2005, p. 51). Regarding corporate crime, authors like Wells assert that corporation operate in a different cultural environment than individuals. Yet not for being different would be less cultural and therefore vulnerable to social control through criminal law. Moreover, criminal law may offer to victims a direct and easier way to compensation. Furthermore, the author argues that

> since many of the victims of corporate wrongdoing are unaware of the source of the harm done to them and therefore cannot invoke the criminal enforcement system as do victims of burglary, there is a state obligation to provide that mechanism for them in the form of proactive investigation backed up by effective sanction.
>
> WELLS, 2001, p. 17

2.4.4 International Standards, Laws, Soft Laws and Comparative Law

As it was mentioned throughout the work, there are several international soft laws and standards that allude to the issue of corporate criminal liability and compliance management systems. Regarding the latter, it can be mentioned the International Organization for Standardization ISO 19600 about Compliance Management Systems (2014), which sets up the main guidelines for establishing and implementing a CMSs (see Figure 1). Moreover, the ISO 13701 (2016) from the same organism, which treats a specific type of system that targets the risk of bribery within the company, thus it launches an Anti-bribery Management System (AMS). Additionally, it can be mentioned the ISO 26000 as Guidance Standard on Social Responsibility (2010).

In the bank sector the Basel Committee on Banking Supervision (BCBS) released in 2005 the document on "Compliance and the Compliance Function in Banks". In that document the BCBS established the purpose of compliance programmes and the function scope of compliance officers. On a more general basis, the G20 released in an annex to the Leaders Declaration a "High Level Principles on the Liability of Legal Persons for Corruption" (2017). In the annex, the leaders recognised the necessity of corporate criminal liability as a tool to fight corruption and encouraged firms to invest in compliance programmes (G20, 2017, p. 2). Moreover, the Organisation for Economic Co-operation and Development released the "G20/OECD Principles of Corporate Governance", where it also recommended the implementation of compliance programmes (OECD, 2015, p. VI.D.7). Additionally, it is also relevant the UN Guiding Principles on Business and Human Rights (2011).

On the European Laws level, the second protocol to the 1997 Convention for the Protection of the Communities' Financial Interests, establishes in its article three that state members ought to ensure that firms are held liable for offences such as fraud, corruption and money laundering. In the same way, the 1999 Criminal Law Convention on Corruption also foresaw the liability of legal persons (with a legal overlapping as it was pointed out by Di Ronco, 2014, p. 27).

On a comparative analysis, Spain first contemplated Corporate Criminal Liability with the article 4 of the Organic Law 5/2010 the 22nd June. That law modified the Criminal Code and introduced the article 31bis which foresaw the corporate criminal liability and the implementation of a CMS, among others, as extenuating circumstance. On the 30th March 2015, the Organic Law number one changed the article 31bis of the criminal code through its article 20. In the newly written article the CMS was contemplated as an exonerating circumstance. On the other hand, Italy introduced the corporate criminal liability through a legislative decree in 2001 that contemplated a generic model of criminal liability (Lavorgna & Di Ronco, 2015, p. 259). Moreover, the decree contemplated in its article six a due diligence as a defence and what is interpreted by due diligence may vary with the particular form of liability (Gobert & Punch, 2003, p. 110). Moreover, the United Kingdom adopted in 2007 the Corporate Manslaughter and Corporate Homicide Act. In its section 8(3) the act enables the jury to consider attitudes, policies, systems or practices within the organisation that might have encouraged any failure. Additionally, the Bribery Act of 2010 foresaw in its section 7(2) as a defence for an organisation to show that it had proper procedures to prevent bribery conducts.

2.5 *Conclusion*

Corporate criminality constitutes a topic of convergence for several fields of knowledge. Drawing on the debates from different theories it was presented a scan on the mainstream criminological trends regarding deviance within an organisational environment. These theories showed an inclination towards a multiple factor analysis regarding social strains (Agnew, 1992). Moreover, the methodological criticism on criminological research from the early twentieth century shifted the focus of analysis towards a more inclusive understanding of deviance (Young, 1981). Within white-collar criminality, the crime-encouraging disorganised structures and the criminal learning through a common environment (Sutherland, 1940, p. 11) led the way to a corporate connection (2.a.iii). This connection helped to create a picture of organisations as comprehensive laboratory cases that could be studied on a micro level.

Furthermore, while corporate studies developed several theories to analyse corporative environments, their aim was always driven by profit and efficiency. Nevertheless, these theories eased the understanding of corporate management and their implementation towards an organisational cultural change (McFarland & Gómez, 2014, p. 97). Moreover, it was introduced the advantage that CSR and CMS could present to firms both from the minimisation of a wide range of risks to the marketing and business opportunities (Spence, 1973). It was not only useful for steering the company but it was also necessary to access new markets through suppliers and clients.

On the other hand, albeit fighting a long-lasting tradition, criminal law found an intrinsic value in corporate criminal liability. It enabled a better law enforcement by complying a self-governance duty on corporations while offering individuals a more proper mean to channel their claims and complains (Wells, 2001). Additionally, it aimed to generate a similar effect that punishment on individuals and thus pursuing the deterrence of corporate misconducts with high potential social impact (Cohen, 1996; Roxin, 1997; Wells, 2001; Mir Puig, 2005).

In this sense, while the international legal trend can be seen to be shifting towards a full recognition of corporate criminal liability there is still a thorough debate on the responsibility attribution models and the way the judicial system ought to consider compliance programmes.

For that matter, this work will focus on a specific socio-legal environment and analyse the way CCL and CMS interact in relation to companies and judicial institutions. This will be done through the content analysis of multiple sources such as judicial acts and interviews with relevant agents. This will allow me to contrast the deontological approach of Law with the ontological perception of the actors who deal with CCL and Compliance in their daily work, as is the case of Compliance Officers. In other words, this work will contrast the crime control goal of criminal justice with the organisational management for efficiency and risk control purpose of companies. The result will shed some light on a not so often researched topic.

3 Methodology

As it was presented in the introduction (1.a) and developed throughout the literature review, the main research questions (RQ) addressed by this work are:

> RQ_1: How have Compliance Management Systems (CMSs) been understood and used by the law to target corporate criminality?
> RQ_2: And, how do CMSs work in different corporations?

This work aims to be mainly exploratory, in opposition to theory-testing (Wengraf, 2001, p. 51). As it was stated by Schnyder and Kern (2015),

> Surprisingly, few researchers have systematically investigated the impact of changing legal rules on corporate governance practices at the firm level. We therefore know comparatively little about what impact recent legal changes had on companies' behaviour and how this affects a country's corporate governance regime as a whole.

For that reason, there is very new and experimental development in this field of knowledge. Moreover, the limited access to data makes every contribution becomes relevant to allow other researchers to see a wider picture. Thus, the exploratory nature of this work aims to give a preliminary mapping on the topic as well as contribute in the development of more solid theoretical grounds.

In that sense, it is worth to consider first the limitations of doing research in this field for it certainly conditioned the chosen method. As it was shown in the literature review, the topic of CCL and CMS as a defence against punishment has taken an international dimension that adds a deep complexity to any research. For that reason, I chose to concentrate on the study of one country to deeply explore how CMS and CCL in one single case. Other reasons were the limitations of researching this topic and the short time I had to conduct it.

Moreover, the chosen methodology was divided into two branches of sources each aiming to address one of the main research questions.

3.1 *Case Study: Spain*

That been said, this work is limited to Spain as a case study (Thomas, 2016, p. 14) of the corporate compliance and corporate liability phenomenon. The Corporate Criminal Liability is contemplated in the Spanish Criminal Code under the article 31bis. This article was introduced through the article four of the Organic Law No. 5/2010 which only foresaw as extenuating circumstances the actions of the firm after a crime. Five years later, the article twenty of the Organic Law No. 1/2015 modified the law of 2010 and introduced as an exculpatory circumstance the previous-to-crime establishment and maintenance of a proper risk based Compliance Management System. Additionally, the decisions of the Supreme Court and the General Attorney's Office on corporate criminal liability, gave the country an attractive edge to consider. In that way, Spain remains at an initial stage in terms of CCL with many institutional decisions still due to be taken, including a clear purpose and the alignment of governmental institutions. That state of affairs constitute the perfect scenario to analyse the way in which a law that contemplates CCL may change the perspective of Companies. Moreover, the fact that Spain is rooted in a Civil Law Tradition with a strong tie to a general theory of crime (Fletcher, 2000, p. 393), adds to the analysis a deeper sense of strain between criminal law and corporate criminal law (Silva Sanchez, 2016, p. 7).

On a more personal level, the fact that I am a Spanish native speaker gives me an advantage when collecting and analysing the data. However, I am not a Spanish citizen. That factor can be evaluated from two different angles. On the one hand, it may provide an advantage for I am not biased by the cultural identity of the people living in that socio-legal environment. On the other hand, it might be a disadvantage for I might have not been able to pick up certain perceptions connected with the national identity and cultural capital (Bourdieu, 1977, p. 187) of the population.

Furthermore, a first approach to the literacy of the law is needed in order to get familiarised with the terminology and the consequences that it contemplates for corporate wrongdoings. Thus, I will mention the legal frames of Spain as well as the consideration of soft laws by judicial authorities. Moreover, the judicial precedents will enable a better understanding of the legal support that regulates corporate activities from the perspective of the judges who oversee its interpretation. It will also show the justification of judges for corporate punishment (Cohen, 1996).

3.2 *Sources of Data*

As it can be seen in Figure 2 the data was divided into two main categories around the case study and in relation to the two RQ: Judicial Acts (RQ_1) and Interviews (RQ_2). At the same time, the judicial acts category was divided according to the judicial institution that issued them. Thus, it encompasses: The General Prosecutor's Opinion (*Circular No. 1/2016*), and the rulings of the Supreme Court after the reform of 2015.

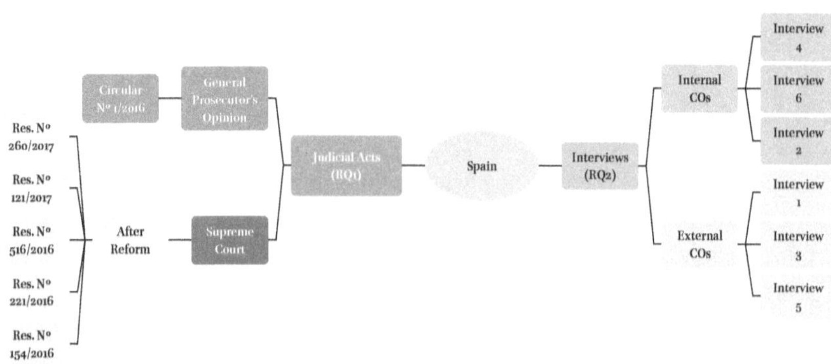

FIGURE 2 Mind Map of research sources and classification

Regarding the interviews, their distinction was made considering if they were internal members of a company or members of a consultant company that provided the services of a Compliance Officer.

3.2.1 Judicial Acts (RQ_1)

For that matter, I searched for case law connected with CCL through the Spanish public database *Centro de Documentación Judicial* (CENDOJ). The search was narrowed down by applying four filters. The first one was related to the jurisdiction (*jurisdicción*) and it was narrowed to only criminal cases (*Penal*). The second one, concerned the type of judgement (*Tipo res.*) and it was selected to search only for judgements (*Sentencia*). The third one involved the type of institution (*Tipo de órgano*) and it was chosen to filter only judgements of the Supreme Court in Criminal matters (*Tribunal Supremo. Sala de lo Penal*). Lastly, the keywords used to limit the search were "corporate criminal liability" and "31 bis" (*"responsabilidad penal de las personas jurídicas" Y "31 bis"*). With these filters, the search threw eight results with the following judgement number (*Nº de Resolución*): 260/2017, 121/2017, 516/2016, 221/2016, 154/2016, 436/2012, 1100/2011 and 547/2011. Finally, I erased all those that were issued before the law reform of 2015, so as to leave the ones that considered the updated legal frame.[1]

On the other hand, I also collected the opinion of the General Prosecutor that was cited in several of the gathered precedents. The position of the General Prosecutor can be hierarchically compared to the judges of the Supreme Court within the Prosecutor's Office as an institution. Thus, his opinion was taken from the Circular No. 1/2016 issued because of the reform of 2015.

Also, this work attempted to deconstruct the objectives of CMS according to the Spanish law and discuss their suitability to generate a change in a corporate sub-culture. In other words, it tried to provide new insight on the corporate view of CMS as tools of social control and thus tried to look for the deterrent effect of imposed CMSs on corporations and individuals. For that purpose, the research was divided in two dimensions of scrutiny. On the one hand, it regarded the relation between the law and the Companies through CMSs and CCL, whilst on the other hand, it focused on the relation between CMSs and the Companies. The main objective was to shed light on the role that criminal law and CMSs plays in the corporate world.

1 The results of the search reflect the output by September 2017.

3.2.2 Interviews (RQ_2)

In order to gain insight on the corporate perspective regarding CCL and CMS, I conducted a series of extended opened interviews with Compliance Officers (CO) in Spain who have a direct contact with the topic. However, the elitist nature of the targeted population (Sarantakos, 2013, p. 279) represented a serious obstacle both when arranging and conducting the interviews. The unique and sensible information CO manage from Companies turns the access to data a very complicated issue. Moreover, it was necessary that the interviewees had a direct contact and experience with the compliance work in Companies (Cresswell & Plano Clark, 2011). For that reason, the main selecting criteria was that they ought to hold a position of Compliance Officers whether it was as an internal member or an external consultant. The importance of this choice relied on the daily work of the interviewees. The crucial information to assess was their perception of their work in relation with the company. Likewise, they were in a position to explain how the law affected their work.

For that reason, the sample consisted of six interviewees who were contacted through three different persons that acted as "gatekeepers" and who had a professional or friendship relation with the participants. Only one participant that gives consulting services as a Compliance Officer was directly contacted thanks to an earlier relation with the author. Although all the participants were or did work as Compliance Officers, two were inside members of a company whilst the rest were members of another firm that offered compliance consulting services for multiple companies.

The chosen interviewees were selected through a process of purposeful sampling (Patton, 2002). As a non-probability sampling method (Sarantakos, 2013, pp. 169–178), the purposeful sample allowed to target participants with fairly rich information (Patton, 2002). As it was pointed out at the beginning of this chapter, the targeted population consisted on a small elite, which made the availability another decisive factor for choosing a purposeful sampling method (Palinkas, et al., 2013, p. 534; Sarantakos, 2013, p. 279). As it was suggested in other study (Maramwidze-Merrison, 2016, p. 159), elites tend to erect barriers around themselves making harder to conduct a proper sampling process.

The first participant is a member of a law firm which provides compliance services to companies (Interview 1, 2017). As he answered during the interview, his firm has gambling companies as its main clients but also offers services to companies in other sectors, such as energy. The second interview took place with internal members of a concession and construction company that works on a multinational level with headquarters in Spain. The interview was conducted with the Head of Compliance and a member of his team. The third interview was also conducted with an external consultant member of a law firm that offers compliance services to other companies. Moreover, this participant was a former judge of a hierarchically high court. The fourth interview was held with the Head of Compliance of one of the top five Banks in Spain (Karwacki, 2015). At the beginning of this interview the participant did not consent to audiotape it. For that reason, thorough notes were taken during and after the meeting. The fifth interview was performed with a member of a consultant law firm which provides compliance services to other companies. Moreover, the participant is a well renowned scholar in the Compliance field. Finally, the last interview was held via "Skype" with the Head of Compliance of one of the most important Spanish gambling companies.

The type of interview employed was semi-structured. While the interviews were conducted with a list of open-ended questions, the wording and order were changed according to the circumstances of the interviews allowing for probes and follow-ups (Sarantakos, 2013, p. 278). The question list was used as a guide to keep a constant flow of topics during the interview. Thus, it enabled the participant to expand on certain issues, clarify others and provide their perceptions more freely and in a, sometimes achieved, informal environment.

All the interviews were conducted in person, in Spain, that is to say face to face. The only exception was interview number six which was taken through the software "Skype". Moreover, the interviews were audiotaped with the verbal consent of the participant, except for one who refused. However, that participant allowed to take notes which were added together with the transcription of the rest. Additionally, all the participants were informed about the voluntary nature of the interviews and were notified of their anonymization as well as the anonymization of all its content and reference in the final work. They were also informed about the security of the audiotape as well as the persons who could access it. Concordantly, all the participants gave their full verbal consent to take part in the research.

3.3 *Data Analysis*

Both the interviews and the judicial acts were examined through the content analysis of the documents and transcripts. For that purpose, I used the software NVivo for Mac, version 11.4.1 (2079). The implementation of word frequency analysis was used in some instances to confirm the relevance of the chosen nodes. Moreover, it will be presented the coverage of each node in order to show the weight of the topic along the source.

Considering the sampling limitations and the fact that this work consists, on a macro level, in a case study, it is necessary to point out the impossibility of generalising the results (Thomas, 2016, p. 17). In the same way, there is a vast amount of research on each individual topic descripted in the literature review such as white-collar criminality, organisational behaviour, corporate governance, or corporate criminal law. However, there is very little research on their interaction (Di Ronco, 2014; Lavorgna & Di Ronco, 2015) as it is presented throughout this work. For that reason, this study aims to shed some light or give a preliminary mapping on the relation between CCL and CMSs (Wengraf, 2001, p. 51; Thomas, 2016, p. 126).

4 Analysis

This chapter will be divided into the two categories of sources each discussing one of the RQs. Additionally, a first approach to the data was necessary to give a basic map regarding the CCL and CMS in Spain. Therefore, whilst the judicial acts and precedents will address the issue of how CMS have been understood and used by the law, the interviews will try to analyse the way CMS work in different firms. The data was studied using content analysis with the help of NVivo. Thus, the information was divided into nodes that gave the data different edges from where to see the topics.

4.1 *Spain's Legal Frame*

As it was already mentioned in chapter 2.5, the CCL was developed in Spain with the article four of the Organic Law 5/2010. This law introduced the article 31 bis that was later modified with the Organic Law 1/2015. Thus, the Criminal Code establishes in the relevant fragments of article 31 bis in its First Book (General Part), that legal persons will be liable of crimes committed on their behalf whether it represent a direct or indirect benefit to them. Additionally, it asserts that the persons acting on behalf of the company could be their legal representatives, persons acting individually or as member of a body within the company. Moreover, it states that a company will be liable of the offences committed by those persons subjected to their authority whose conduct was enabled by a gross breach of the supervision, surveillance and control duties of the organisation.

Furthermore, section two of the article states the conditions under which legal persons may be exempted of liability. In that sense, the legal person has to implement a prior-to-crime model of organisation management with proper tools to prevent crimes within the organisation. It shall foresee measures of monitoring and control as well as a crime risk assessment considering the activities of the company. The entrusted person to carry out the organisational management must have autonomous power of initiative regarding control and monitoring. Finally, the individual offender must commit the crime by evading the controls of the organisation.

Moreover, the article 31 bis establishes a system of *numerus clausus* where companies can be liable of the crimes that specifically foresee the CCL option (General Prosecutor's Office of Spain, 2016, p. 4). Thus, in addition to be complemented by the article 129 regarding other types of Legal Persons, the article 31 bis is also complemented with the corporate related offences of the second book of the criminal code, which specifies every criminal behaviour.

4.2 *Judicial Acts*

As it is shown in figure 3, in order to perform the content analysis, the source was deconstructed (Cohen, 2001, p. 228) into three nodes: Compliance Management Systems, Liability Models, and Reasons for the genesis of CCL. At the same time, the CMSs node was split into ontology of CMSs and Purpose of CMSs. The first one referred to those statements concerning what is a CMSs, what makes a management programme be a compliance management program and not some other programme. The latter covered the goals of CMSs according to the Attorney General.

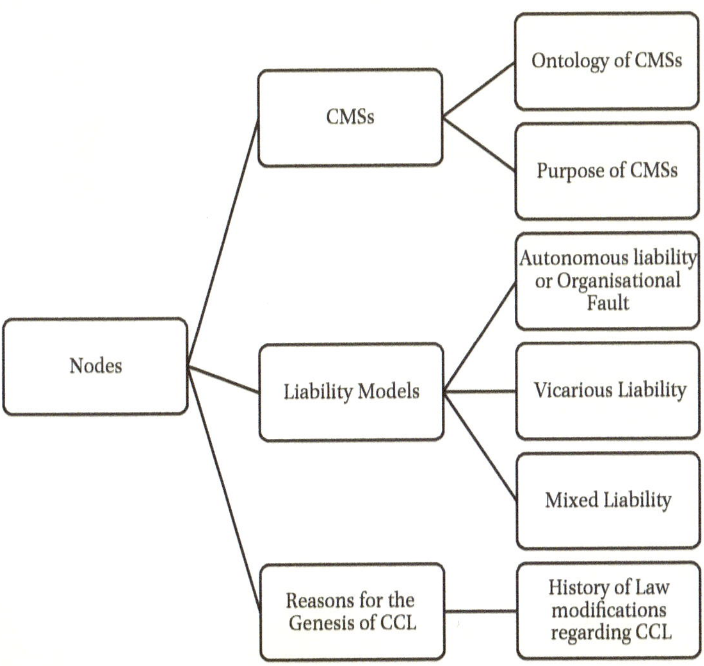

FIGURE 3 Nodes of the source "General Prosecutor's Opinion"

Regarding the node on liability models, it was divided into the three main models referred in the Spanish literature. In that sense, the first two were already mentioned in chapter 2.4.2. The model of mixed liability, on the other hand, asserts that while the article 31 bis 1(a) contemplated the vicarious liability, on the other hand, model, the section 1(b) suggested an inclination towards the organisational fault model (General Prosecutor's Office of Spain, 2016, p. 6).

Also, the node on the reasons for the genesis of CCL was integrated by those references to why did CCL develop in Spain and how did it evolve in the country.

4.2.1 General Prosecutor's Opinion

The title of the source is "about the criminal liability of legal persons according to the reform of the Criminal Code introduced by the Organic Law 1/2015". In this document, the General Prosecutor at that time was Consuelo Madrigal Martínez-Pereda. Through that Circular she addressed the rest of the prosecutors to clarify certain interpretation aspects concerning CCL. Although her interpretation of the law is not mandatory neither for district attorneys nor for judges, it represents an authoritative opinion from the highest hierarchical position within the institution of Prosecutors.

TABLE 1 Node's coverage of General Prosecutor's Opinion

Nodes	References	Coverage
Ontology of CMSs	36	6.73%
Purpose of CMSs	16	2.14%
Autonomous Liability or Organisational Fault	6	1.57%
Mixed Liability	1	0.42%
Vicarious Liability	13	1.97%
Reasons for the Genesis of CCL	7	1.49%
History of Law Modifications Regarding CCL	2	0.66%

TABLE 2 Word count of the 15 most frequent words in the General Prosecutor's Opinion with a minimum length of 5 characters[2]

Word	Count	Weighted percentage	Similar words
Persons	334	1.52%	person, persons
Legal	259	1.18%	juridical, legal
Liability	184	0.84%	responsibility, responsibilities
Crime	139	0.63%	crime, crimes
Criminal	125	0.57%	penal, criminals
Model	123	0.56%	model, models
Controls	108	0.49%	control, controls
General	95	0.43%	general, generals
Paragraph	92	0.42%	paragraph, paragraphs
Organisation	84	0.38%	organisation
State	78	0.35%	state, states
Prosecutor's Office	65	0.30%	Prosecutor's Office
Management	56	0.25%	management
Compliance	50	0.23%	fulfilment
Commit	45	0.20%	commission

As table 2 shows, the most frequent words used were "Persons" and "Legal". That can be justified through the extensive explanation of what constituted a legal person according to the Spanish law, topic that exceeds the scope of this work. Moreover, the word count of Paragraph can be explained by the constant reference to the sections of the Spanish law, for the purpose of the whole document is to clarify its interpretation. That been said, the rest of the most frequent words relate directly with the nodes in table 1, thus confirming their relevancy.

4.2.1.1 *Compliance Management Systems*

As table 1 shows, the text focused mainly in the explanation of Compliance Programmes or CMSs as well as the purpose of them. In that sense, the Prosecutor criticised the introduction of the requirements that a CMS ought to have to be recognised by the criminal justice. She established that

2 Own translation from the original in Spanish.

> The programs involve demands of a corporate nature. Their own corporate organizational structure require a high degree of development and **have a clear preventive purpose**, reasons that should have brought this regulation to the corresponding mercantile legislation. If that was the case, the judge could turn to it to assess the existence of an organization adequate to prevent crimes in the company, in a similar way as what happens with the regulations for the prevention of money laundering and the financing of terrorism
>
> GENERAL PROSECUTOR'S OFFICE OF SPAIN, 2016, p. 39, emphasis added

In that sense, the document referred to several points that needed to be present in order to consider a CMS fit for exculpating the company. Therefore, it asserts that the criminal justice procedure encompasses the suitability evaluation of the CMS adopted by the firm (General Prosecutor's Office of Spain, 2016, p. 38).

Although the technical details exceed the scope of this work, it is worth mentioning some of the main requirements emphasised in the opinion of the General Prosecutor. In the first place, compliance programmes must be written, clear, precise and effective. It is not sufficient to just have a compliance programme, it should also proof to be adequate to prevent the concrete offence of which the firm is being charged (General Prosecutor's Office of Spain, 2016, p. 43). The document points out the dubious practice of copying the compliance programmes of other organisations. It highlights that doing so would cast serious doubt on the effectiveness of the programme and the real commitment of the senior members to prevent criminal behaviours (General Prosecutor's Office of Spain, 2016, p. 43).

Furthermore, it stablishes that the CMS must be risk based and identify the risks according to clients, countries and geographic areas (General Prosecutor's Office of Spain, 2016, p. 43). It also must contemplate the nature of operations handled by the company and take into consideration the expended time in them. Likewise, the circular stresses the importance of instituting a channel of complains together with a detailed procedure of whistle-blower protection. This would increase the trust of employees and enable the senior managers to have a better flow of information that would eventually allow prevention or the adoption of adequate measures (General Prosecutor's Office of Spain, 2016, p. 45). Regarding these measures, the General Prosecutor affirmed the duty to set up a disciplinary system to sanction the behaviours against the norms of the compliance programme (General Prosecutor's Office of Spain, 2016, p. 45). The company should also demand a deep commitment with the corporate ethic culture from the senior members. This commitment sets an example to other members and contributes to the creation of the compliance ethical culture (General Prosecutor's Office of Spain, 2016, pp. 52, 63).

Regarding the purpose of CMSs, while the earlier quote referred to the administrative nature of the CMSs, it gave a hint on its "preventive purpose". However, this practical rationale seems to be required in parallel with a moral goal. Thus,

> In essence, the organizational and management models or corporate compliance programs are not intended to make companies avoid criminal sanctions. They are intended to promote a true corporate ethics culture. The company must have a model to comply with legality in general and, of course, with criminal law but not only with it. This was the only content that the 2015 Legislator expressly imposes on organisational and management models. It still restricts its application scope more by limiting that kind of criminal compliance to "crimes of the same nature"
>
> GENERAL PROSECUTOR'S OFFICE OF SPAIN, 2016, p. 39

Therefore, according to the General Prosecutor, CMSs may play three non-exclusive roles. In relation to the company a CMS may be established as a way to avoid criminal charges. It may also be instituted as a mean to prevent criminal behaviours within the firm by minimising the risks. Lastly, it can be introduced as a tool to promote a corporate ethic culture. However, the CMS would not be valid to the criminal justice if it is only introduced by the company just to avoid criminal charges. In other words, the particular CMS must be connected with the reality of the Company.

Furthermore, the opinion of the General Prosecutor points out those cases in which the offence brings a secondary benefit to the corporation, thus remaining as an individual offence with an individual purpose. The Prosecutor asserts that in those cases the deterrent effect of a CMS would be scarce, even when it is properly established and improved. Even more, the threat of punishment from the corporation would not represent a bigger threat, to the individual, than the punishment of the criminal justice (General Prosecutor's Office of Spain, 2016, p. 53). For that reason, The General Prosecutor advised the rest of state attorneys to "value in a special way that the organization and control models of the company establish high ethical standards in the hiring and promotion of managers and employees" (General Prosecutor's Office of Spain, 2016, p. 53). Thus, on top of the duty of adequate election of suitable and ethical members there is the duty of proper delegation of work and surveillance.

4.2.1.2 *Liability*

The second group of nodes coverage encompassed the three main models of liability considered by the Spanish literature on CCL (Silva Sanchez, 2016, p. 285): vicarious liability, organisational fault or autonomous, and mixed model of liability.

The Opinion of the General Prosecutor clearly states that

> The Organic Law 1/2015 maintains in letters a) and b) of art. 31 bis the essential foundation of attribution of criminal responsibility to the legal person *through a vicarious type or by representation.* Both sections of article 31 bis demand, in the same way as before the reform, the previous commission of an offense by a natural person in the concrete circumstances that are established in the Criminal Code. The first fact of connection between corporation and individual is generated by people with greater responsibilities in the entity and the second by people unduly controlled by those.
>
> GENERAL PROSECUTOR'S OFFICE OF SPAIN, 2016, pp. 5, 58, emphasis added

Moreover, the interpretation of the law as contemplating the other two models of CCL is harshly criticised to maintain the interpretation of the law according to which it imposes a vicarious model of liability for corporations. In that sense, the mixed model of liability would sustain a vicarious liability for section 1(a) of the article 31 bis, while the section 1(b) of it supported the organisational fault model. However, "this suggestive interpretation is not in accordance with the wording of the precept, neither in its initial wording before the reform nor in the current one with the Organic Law 1/2015" (General Prosecutor's Office of Spain, 2016, p. 6).

Regarding the organizational fault model, the document affirms that if the liability relied in the organization or lack of it, a compliance programme would be an objective element of the offence. Thus, this element would be part of the *actus reus* constituting a case of *mala quia prohibita* (Goldstein & Goldstein, 1971, p. 328). If that were the case, the existence of a CMS would eliminate the offence in itself rather than exonerating the firm from responsibility. Nevertheless, the document recognizes that other articles in the criminal code such as 31 ter or 31 quater may lead to think of an organizational fault model of liability. Despite that, it asserts that such a model would also demand a corporate state of mind or *mens rea*, something that is still not required by the Spanish Law (General Prosecutor's Office of Spain, 2016, pp. 8–9).

4.2.1.3 *Genesis of CCL*

Regarding the perceived reasons for the introduction of the CCL in the Spanish criminal code, the General Prosecutor asserted that it was a product "of the incessant process of international harmonization of Criminal Law and of the felt need to give a more effective response to the advance of corporate criminality" (General Prosecutor's Office of Spain, 2016, p. 1). Moreover, it stablishes that the CCL was born as a complement of the individual liability, imposed not to help this last one evade criminal sanctions but so as not to leave criminals without punishment.

On the other hand, when referring to the history of CCL law modifications the General Prosecutor attributed the Organic Law 1/2015 the goal of clarifying certain misunderstandings of the previous CCL law of 2010.

4.2.2 Case Law

TABLE 3 Nodes coverage of Supreme Court's precedents

Nodes/Precedents	154/2016	221/2016	516/2016	121/2017	260/2017
Ontology of CMSs	-	-	-	-	-
Purpose of CMSs	0.18%	0.08%	-	-	-
Autonomous Liability or Organisational Fault	0.17%	-	-	0.21%	-
Mixed Liability	1.38%	1.11%	-	-	-
Vicarious Liability	1.21%	-	1.49%	-	-
Reasons for the Genesis of CCL	-	-	-	-	-
History of Law Modifications Regarding CCL	-	-	-	-	-

When considering this source it is worth mentioning that a word count would not reveal any relevant data for the topic of this research. This is because case laws ideally represent a debate between three parties. In other words, there are many topics being discussed that not necessarily relate with CCL or CMS, such as procedural rights and proof standards, among others. That can explain the lack of nodes in Res. 260/2017, for it mentions CCL to explain that because the offence was committed in 2006, the law of 2010 which contemplates CCL cannot be applied (Res. 260/2017, p. 12).

That been said, while the nodes for this source were kept the same as in the Opinion of the General Prosecutor, the results focused mainly on the liability models. This can be explained through the duty of the judges to consider and justify the liability of a firm before funding it guilty and imposing a punishment or funding it not guilty and acquitting.

4.2.2.1 *Compliance*

In that sense, CMSs were mentioned principally in precedents 154/2016 and 221/2016. Regarding the first, judges established that the surveillance and control measures called compliance models have the goal of preventing criminal behaviour within the organisation (Res. No. 154/2016, p. 63). With the same argument, the Res. No. 221/2016 asserted that the mechanisms of control and management have preventive system called to avoid criminal behaviours within the organisation (Res. No. 221/2016, p. 43).

4.2.2.2 *Liability*

Regarding liability models, precedents have not had a clear and unanimous opinion on the legal interpretation that grounds the CCL. In that sense, the Res. No. 154/2016 was a deeply contingent ruling. The decision was adopted with eight out of fifteen judges affirming that the Organic Law 1/2015 adopted a mixed liability model. Moreover, it recalls the preamble of the law where the lawmaker affirms that the new law "puts an end to the interpretative doubt casted by some scholars who interpreted the norm as regarding a vicarious liability model" (Res. No. 154/2016, p. 64).

Furthermore, eight out of fifteen judges in this ruling established that the new law requires the firm to prove they possess a compliance culture through a CMS. However, that requisite would imply a strict liability without a state of mind or *mens rea*, postulation that is not compatible with the vicarious liability model, expressly rejected by the lawmaker (Res. No. 154/2016, p. 64). Thus, this majority of judges interpreted the liability model chosen by the Spanish law to be a mixed liability model. They emphasise that

> What does not admit any doubt is that the system of corporate criminal liability is grounded on the previous verification of a crime committed by an individual, member of the organisation. Additionally, it requires the establishment and correct application of efficient control measures aiming to prevent and avoid, when possible, criminal behaviours from the members of the organisation.
>
> Res. No. 154/2016, p. 61

On the other hand, seven out of fifteen judges in the case law understood that the standard of proving the lack of a compliance culture is vague and against the certainty principle of law. They asserted that even though a compliance culture is the ultimate ground for a CCL, as the respect for life is the ground for punishing homicide, a CMS would not be part of the objective element or *actus reus* of the corporate crime (Res. No. 154/2016, p. 96).

In that sense, while the Res. No. 221/2016 also advocated for a mixed liability model requiring a previous individual crime (Res. No. 221/2016, p. 43), the Res. 516/2016 seems to support the vicarious liability interpretation. Therefore, it says that "when analysing the Corporate Criminal Liability, the lawmaker opted for a vicarious liability system, being independent the criminal responsibility of the natural person and the legal person [...], each answering of their own responsibility" (Res. No. 516/2016, p. 6). On the other hand, while the Res. No. 260/2017 does not mention anything regarding liability, the Res. No. 121/2017 appears to uphold an autonomous or organizational fault model. In that sense, it stablishes that "the criminal responsibility of the legal person does not condition that of the natural person, nor vice versa" (Res. No. 121/2017, p. 4). This assertion would seem to indicate that it would not be necessary to confirm the crime of the individual to be able to find a corporation liable, thus indicating an autonomous liability of the organisation.

4.3 *Interviews*

In the first place, the interviews are numerated chronologically as they were conducted. For analysis purposes, as illustrated in figure 4, all the translations were divided into four nodes: Goals of CCL; Reasons for Setting a CMS; Management Procedures; and Perceived Trends.

In that sense, the node "Goals of CCL Laws" referred to the perceptions of the participants in relation to what do they think the Law aimed to accomplish by imposing the CCL. On the other hand, the node "Reasons for Setting a CMS" encompassed all the benefits that a CMS would bring to an organisation as well as the motivations beyond benefits they might have to set a CMS. It also refers to the perceived goals of a CMS may that be in relation to the law, for example avoiding criminal charges; or in relation to the company, for example boosting efficiency and production. The node "Management Procedures" includes all the processes and measures that are foresee by the CMS, such as punishments, hotlines for complaints, trainings, among others. Finally, the "Perceived Trends" node addresses the participant's perception on future developments or concerns in the world of Compliance. This node includes perceptions

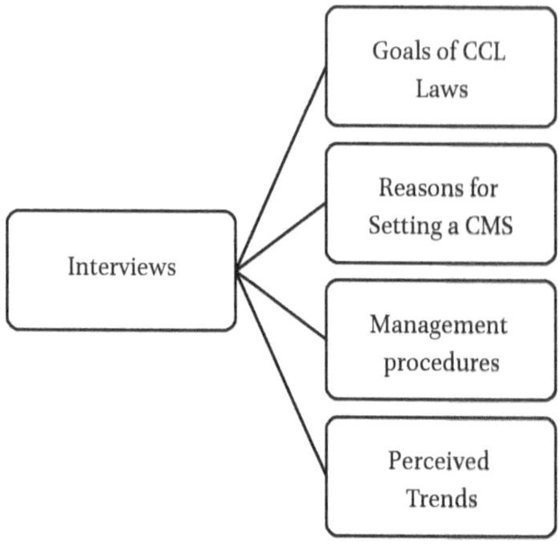

FIGURE 4 Nodes of source: Interviews

regarding the law, the companies and the future of CMS itself, such as a new software, new tools, union problems, judicial issues, etc.

In that sense, table 4 shows the coverage and references of all the interviews divided by the aforementioned nodes. As it can be seen, the nodes "Reasons for Setting a CMS" and "Management Procedures" received the highest coverage.

4.3.1 Reasons for Setting a CMS

Regarding this node, the respondents showed a deep connection between CMS and business opportunities. They relied in the benefits that CMSs could bring to companies and perceived that benefit as the main reason for setting a CMS. By using phrases such as: "a gambling company is worth as much as the legality

TABLE 4 Nodes coverage of interviews

Nodes	Interview 1		Interview 2		Interview 3	
	References	Coverage	References	Coverage	References	Cover
Goals of CCL Laws	5	4.99%	3	14.39%	4	17.17%
Reasons for setting a CMS	12	22.62%	8	22.25%	6	21.60%
Management Procedures	6	18.81%	5	16.19%	6	26.83%
Perceived Trends	2	5.24%	1	24.50%	1	10.76%

of its licences" (Interview 1, 2017, answer 4), they reaffirmed the connection between compliance with the law and economic benefits.

On the other hand, when asked about the perception of what an organisation looked for when implementing a CMS, the answers were:

> I believe that it gives legal security, the company says I am here, I want to do business following the law, I have a commitment to comply with the law and anyone who is not on board can leave. That is the advantage. From my point of view this increases the value of companies and makes it easier to buy the companies if you are going to sell your company and you have a compliance plan, and you have well-articulated and well organised, your company is worth more. It is easier to sell it: look here is everything I have and everything is perfect.
>
> INTERVIEW 1, 2017, answer 17

Following the same logic, the respondent said that,

> Companies what they have to get are benefits, when do they implement compliance plans? When they have proven or are almost certain, they analyse their risks and say, I am interested in having a compliance plan because I will be able to invest in the United States, or I will do this other thing.
>
> INTERVIEW 1, 2017, answer 17

Moreover, the respondent pointed out future hypothetical benefits of CMS in terms of business opportunities such as new markets or less insurance fee:

Interview 4		Interview 5		Interview 6	
nces	Coverage	References	Coverage	References	Coverage
	11.13%	4	15.56%	1	1.38%
	22.81%	4	22.03%	10	15.62%
	40.57%	4	26.68%	10	21.31%
	8.21%	1	14.84%	2	7.38%

> It generates opportunities, effectively. There are rumours that not only the insurance companies may lower their fee to companies with CMS. There are also rumours that when contracting with the public administration, their requirements for contracting will also demand compliance.
>
> INTERVIEW 1, 2017, answer 18

In the same way, in Interview 6 the participant considered that the main reason his company contemplated when setting a CMS was the business opportunities in new markets. He said

> I'll tell you the essence of why my company needed a Compliance Officer. The company wanted to enter the United States, specifically in Puerto Rico. It wanted to buy a racecourse to establish a gaming concessionaire. In order to do that, the Government of Puerto Rico, like all the American States, does a due diligence to see if you fulfil what they understand by good governance. In other words, the norms of compliance.
>
> INTERVIEW 6, 2017, answer 1

The second interview offered a similar insight when it was said that,

> Two things really happen: one, which materialises the risk, that is, we want to avoid having to face the negative consequences; and then on the other hand bring value. So, our idea, what is it? That if we do have a true compliance culture we can generate a differential value over our competitors that allows us to compete better, allowing us to be more efficient.
>
> INTERVIEW 2, 2017, answer 5

In the same way, during the Interview 3, the respondent asserted that the businessman wanted to sell his product, and thus in order to motivate a compliant behaviour there needs to be a paradigm shift from punishment to profit. Thus, he said that,

> The argument in practice is, let us not talk about sanction, let us talk about it from the pocket. If you want to sell your goods and products, you need a compliance program. That, in addition to everything else: from the financial point of view, obtaining better credits and better rates; better ratings of interest; greater control over the corporation; and an improved ethical climate within the company.
>
> INTERVIEW 3, 2017, answer 6

4.3.2 Management Procedures

In this node, the respondents stressed out the importance of risk assessment to create a proper compliance programme (Interview 1, 2017, answers 5 and 10), thus showing they perceive a connection between CMSs and crime prevention.

In this sense, the respondent in Interview 1 based a good CMS in the commitment of senior managements and a meticulous delineation of each positions function (Interview 1, 2017, answer 11). Finally, he highlighted the importance of hotlines and sanctions. Regarding the latter he said "If it is proven that there is an individual who has been taking money from sales or cheating on purchases or using bribes to get contracts and so and you do not fire him, it is over" (Interview 1, 2017, answer 22).

Moreover, when addressing the hotlines he connected its importance with the flow of information. He affirmed that the hotline "is one of the key elements of the compliance plan because that is where you will find out if something happens or if there is any relevant issue that needs to be addressed" (Interview 1, 2017, answer 14).

In the same way, the participant in Interview 2 discussed the issue of the information flow along the necessity to show that the Compliance Department brings in an aggregated value. Because "if you do not help, if you annoy once they will get angry, if you annoy twice they will get pissed, and for the third one you will not be informed. Directly" (Interview 2, 2017, answer 15).

Regarding the way to generate a desired culture within an organisation, the participant in Interview 5 said,

> That culture, and this is one of the most important legs of a compliance program, is generated with training. Almost everything is generated with training. In fact, even before identifying risks, it is convenient to train the company in what is a model of crime prevention: what it means; what is important, so that everyone can collaborate.
>
> INTERVIEW 5, 2017, answer 6

On the other hand, one issue that called my attention was that three respondents acknowledge illegal activities or breach of contracts in pursuit of fulfilling their duty or keeping the company in business. Thus, Interview 2 showed the participant stating that it should also be consider the right of the company not to comply. The respondent exemplified with a hypothetical 100.000.000 euros contract which holds a section stating a condition impossible to meet by the company but that supposes a minimum impact, so it agrees anyway. To justify that behaviour the respondent said that the legal counselling companies do it all the time and that "of course there is the culture of compliance, but what we cannot do is block the Companies" (Interview 2, 2017, answer 15). In the same way, the participant in the Interview 4 said, "I am sure that there are people who do money laundering in the main financial institutions of the world, what is intended is to avoid an inappropriate behaviour, to handle that risk" (Interview 4, 2017). Finally, the respondent in Interview 6, affirmed

> with the legal tools that were in Spain, no one could reach the chief criminals, except that you forge [evidence], and that is the path that I have taken the most, as I said in my thesis, and I have said publicly now that almost all the counterfeiting I could have done have reached the statute of limitation.
>
> INTERVIEW 6, 2017, answer 1

This information provides some insight on the role of legality and the concept of useful illegality mentioned in chapter 2.4.1.

4.3.3 Perceived Trends

When asked about the future measures that would be needed for companies to properly implement CMSs one participant answered that,

> It will depend on the stick. It will depend a lot on the stick. As soon as they convict four societies; there is continued jurisprudence; and we see clearly how the exoneration works, let us see how the principles of commitment to ethical practices are interpreted, and there we will how companies implement or not CMSs.
>
> INTERVIEW 1, 2017, answer 16

Comparing this last answer with the earlier ones, it might indicate a contradiction between the perceived deterrent effect of punishment and the motives for companies to implement a CMS.

Despite that, some participants identified trends in future regulations of benefits such as the possibility of contracting with the public sector (Interview 2, 2017, answer 8), thus connecting again compliance with profitability. On the same line but aiming for a procedure to shelter the company from the harmful reputational effects of criminal justice, the participant in Interview 3 identified as future trends with alternative methods of conflict resolution such as mediation (Interview 3, 2017, answer 12). On the contrary, the participant in Interview 5, identified as a future trend the procedure strategy towards facing a criminal justice procedure (Interview 5, 2017, answer 10).

On an operational level, Interview 4 focused on the independence of compliance sectors within companies and the impact of new techonologies and technological consecuences such as Big Data (Interview 4, 2017). On the other hand, the participant in Interview 6 highlighted as a future trend the introduction of detectives, policemen and intelligence agents in the world of corporate compliance (Interview 6, 2017, answer 10).

4.3.4 Goals of CCL Laws

In this sense, most of the participants agreed on the need for more time to pass by in order to see the effects of the criminal law on companies. However, some of the participants gave the law a secondary role, reducing its importance. For example, it was affirmed: "I take the law to the background. The important thing is to manage that risk. With terrorism, for example, the level of management changed. I seek compliance to manage risk and only with that I comply with the law" (Interview 4, 2017).

Additionally, the participant in Interview 2 characterised the CCL laws as,

> two sides of a coin because what they tell you is: you cannot receive the capital from outside the financial circuit that are not controlled, but to make sure that you do not do that we give you the other side of the coin, that is to say that you have to fulfill these obligations and if you fulfill the obligations, [...] then we exempt you.
>
> INTERVIEW 2, 2017, answer 3

5 Discussion

5.1 *Research Question 1*

As appears from the content analysis, this RQ may not have a single and straightforward answer. On the contrary, the encountering positions of the two institutions of criminal justice may reveal a lack of clarity in the way the law addressed the issue of CCL and CMS. As it was presented, both the General Prosecutor and the judges of the Supreme Court had different opinions on the judicial nature of CMS and the liability model chosen by the lawmaker. That is to say, that while the rulings and opinions coincide on the preventive exegesis of CMS they differed on the way the judicial system ought to value them, as well as their consequences. That conflict of interpretation can also be seen in the tight majority of judges that subscribed to the first precedent after the reform of 2015 (Res. No. 154/2016, 2016). The principal causes of debate were the operational details regarding the criminal procedure and the location of CCL and CMS in a general theory of crime.

Despite that discussion, the CMS was interpreted by the criminal justice institutions as mainly imposed for preventive purposes. There was also a moral/retributivist reason of not leaving unpunished actors that contributed to certain crimes, like legal persons, and its practical consequence of not letting individuals shelter under the vail of corporations. Moreover, a symbolic approach trusted punishment to generate a deterrent effect in organisations by making them adopt the necessary measures to minimise their risks. In that sense, the symbolic reason connected punishment with CMS and their minimisation of hazards.

To incentive companies to manage their risks and minimise the hazards of their activities the Spanish law adopted a punishment and reward tactic. The latter consisting on the exemption of the first one. However, this instrumental approach (Akers & Jennings, 2016, p. 230) cannot yet be confirmed in Spain, for there has not been a major institutional consensus on the requirements for the reward nor the extent of the punishment. On the other hand, the vicarious mean of learning criminal behaviours on a corporative level (Krohn, 1999, p. 464) may have an effect. The lack of clear consequences for certain corporate behaviours may enable the learning of deviant corporate conducts. Moreover, the solution adopted in the Res. No. 154/2016 for example, was applied to a drug trafficking company, thus constituting a flagrant case. For that reason, the case is not susceptible of clarifying the normal cases of organisations with legal goals of legitimate profit that must face the deviant behaviour of an individual member. Thus, from the social-learning theory point of view, corporate criminality may not be properly targeted until there is a clear institutional message.

Related to white-collar criminality as it was described in the Literature Review, this operational confusion could be associated to the lack of standards or conflict of standards which contribute to social disorganisation on a macro-level. In other words, it is this lack of clarity in the interpretation of the norms that could foster disorganisation among companies. That lack of clear standards might influence on a supra-corporation level and contribute to a macro social disorganisation (Sutherland, 1983, p. 255).

Moreover, considering the GST (Agnew, 2016), without a clear message from the institutions there is not an objective parameter to judge situations so the perception of fairness can be distortion. In the same way, the imposition of a proper CMS might be seen as a burden high in magnitude if it is considered the high cost of its implementation. Additionally, while the social control on corporations is in high demand nowadays, its enforcement it is not so clear. This might create a perception of lower social controls. Lastly, the blockage of goals can be inferred from the strain between compliance with law and profitability. Moreover, the high-risk assumptions and seeking profit in hazardous operations where no one else does, may sometimes define a successful businessperson, and thus increasing the pressure.

The corporate citizen may find it hard to adapt and follow the law when there is not a social consensus on normative standards in the local society. When the "rules of the game" are not properly stated, a corporate citizen may not be able to adequate its behaviour. Moreover, in case of strain with internal goals, it would be less motivated to comply with an unclear governmental law over a clear and straightforward purpose of profit.

5.2 *Research Question 2*

On the occupational level (Clinard & Quinney, 1973; Braithwaite, 1985, p. 19), the disorganisation of the corporate social environment (McFarland & Gómez, 2014) may be reflected in the sub-culture of the individuals that constitute it. For that reason, while CMS have been used by the law to create a culture of compliance with the law that manages risk and minimise hazards, its enforcement might be misdirected.

In accordance with the perception on lack of clear consequences, the participant in Interview 5 asserted that recently

> an auditor involved an economic criminal case with Deloitte has simply been acquitted because she just claimed to have a CMS without saying anything else, there was no investigation on that CMS. Therefore, we are going to find the motivated prosecutor that is going to go and see really how that CMS was implemented or the prosecutor that by just showing him a CMS will end the persecution
>
> INTERVIEW 5, 2017, answer 1

Nowadays the question asked by Colonel Vanderbil could be reformulated (see page 7). Thus, instead of pointing out the contradiction between good business and law, the 4th interviewee affirmed to be sure that money laundering was taking place in the principal financial centres of the world but his job was to manage the risk of that occurring. In that sense, a total prevention was seen as a chimeric goal and the law was perceived as less important as the business losses. In the same way, the acknowledgement of the second participant regarding the breach of contract (Interview 2, 2017, answer 15) constitutes an example of useful illegality (Klinkhammer, 2013).

Moreover, the CMS was perceived by most of the respondents as an enabler of business opportunities, most of them exemplifying with the possibility to access new markets such as the USA. Another illustrative example was provided during Interview 6 where the participant asserted that because of the CMS his company was able to buy a better kind of supply that its mexican competidor could not (Interview 6, 2017, answer 3). Furthermore, the benefits of a CMS were also perceived in future hypothetical rumors such as lower insurance fees or access to better bank loans.

In that sense, far from focusing the attention of avoiding liability and contributing to CSR, the latter is seen as just complying with the law and thus closer to Friedman's logic of just procuring to no harm third parties. However, CSR is also perceived with similar logic as Zizek's ethical consumption concept. In other words, CSR is seen more as a marketing strategy for maximising profit through reputation, access to new markets or access to better supplies. Following that argument, from the point of view of the Signaling Theory the CMS can be seen more as a sign to reduce the information gap and increase the reputation of the company through trust and social responsibility. In other words, it helps to provide an image of a good corporate citizen.

In that way, the CMS as a requirement to access new or better business opportunities may be considered as better motivators than punishment. The positive stimuli of requiring certain acts to enable opportunities may prove more effective than the negative threat of punishment. Moreover, when considering punishment there is another variable to consider. The probability of getting caught, relativizes the effectiveness of the threat (Cohen, 1996), while the requirement interacts with the company ex ante. With the requirement there is no probability, no speculation, and no other variable than the compulsory action to enable the business opportunity.

6 Conclusion

By analysing the case of Spain this work aimed to show some clarifying features of how CMSs could be implemented to target corporate criminality. Moreover, it tried to show how CMSs were implemented by corporations to generate a compliance culture among their members. In this sense, while the legal purpose of demanding a CMS is centred on crime prevention, this work showed a more selfish motive from the organisations side. In other words, rather than focusing on crime prevention and CSR, organisations sought to prevent their own harm and maximise their benefits.

While this may not be considered something new, the analysis of Judicial Acts showed that the benefits of CMS for the company in terms of business opportunities were underexploited by justice. Moreover, the information presented throughout this work may support a stronger sense of effectiveness when applying other means rather than Criminal Justice.

Still, when considering a symbolic purpose of punishment, the deterrent effect may not be accomplished through unclear legislative messages and rarely materialised threats. The law may need to adapt and force methods that hold higher chances of motivating individuals and organisations. A way of aligning the mores of corporate subcultures and the goals of law may be through the motivational power of positive stimuli such as the power of requirements. In that sense, as the interviews showed, the reward for an action may be a stronger source of incentive than the threat of punishment. The fact that participants highlighted the access to new markets and better supplies together with insurance fee discounts as reasons to establish CMSs, implied that those benefits inflicted a stronger sense of motivation.

While this may rule out the traditional purpose of criminal law to prevent corporate criminality, it may lift the importance of administrative or civil law. In other words, punishment may not have as stronger deterrent effect as the requirements to access a market or the requirements to acquire an administrative authorisation to open a business.

Nonetheless, results also showed a relevant concern about the reputational consequences of the criminal procedure and the resulting harm to their gains over the threat of punishment. Thus, criminal law may find a stronger deterrent effect through the criminal procedure rather than through the symbolic purpose of punishment. This idea could support seeking for better results by implementing alternative methods of conflict resolution such as mediation.

The interviews also showed a recycling of resources instead of a proper investment on CMSs. This may also support the idea that corporations do not perceive CSR as altruistic actions but as a mere abiding of law, thus supporting the CSR view of Friedman (1970).

Concordantly with previous research (Lavorgna & Di Ronco, 2015; Di Ronco, 2014), it was not clear that CMSs were a suitable tool to effectivly prevent crime within the organisation. Moreover, interviews showed better results as a tool to manage internal procedures and allign individual goals with corporate goals. While this may be effective on preventing occupational crimes, it may not be so with corporate crimes.

Regarding the limitations, this work was not able to generalise for it consisted mainly on a case study. As mentioned in the methodology, the difficulties concerning the population studied presented a major obstacle for this research. Moreover, there was an initial attempt to perform a comparative analysis between Spain and the United Kingdom. However, it was only possible to access one participant in the latter. Thus, future research could aim to replicate this study in other socio-legal environments and perform a comparative study.

Acknowledgement

I wish to express my sincere gratitude to Professor Valsamis Mitsilegas and Dr Saskia Hufnagel for their mentoring and guidance through my academic endeavours. Also, thanks to Dr Anna Di Ronco, for all the patience and amazing advice when things seemed overwhelming; and Dr Anna Sergi for her counselling and encouragement.

Special gratitude to Professors Mirentxu Corcoy Bidasolo, Jesús María Silva-Sánchez, José Ignacio Gallego Soler, Mariona Llobet Anglí and Raquel Montaner Fernández for their lectures in the University of Barcelona and University Pompeu Fabra, they have been an inspiration for this work.

I would also like to thank my family: Hugo, Claudia and Guga for all the love and support through the years, everything is for and because of you. To my fiancée, Fiore, I have nothing but words of amusement, gratitude, love and admiration; thanks for all the patience and support, thanks for all the tenderness and affection.

Works Cited

Agnew, R., 1992. Foundation for a General Strain Theory of Crime and Delinquency. *Criminology*, 30(1), pp. 47–87.

Agnew, R., 2001. Building on the Foundation of General Strain Theory: Specifying the Types of Strain Most Likely to Lead to Crime and Delinquency. *Journal of Research in Crime and Delinquency*, 1 January, 38(4), pp. 319–361.

Agnew, R., 2012. Reflection on "A Revised Strain Theory of Delinquency". *Social Forces*, 91(1), pp. 33–38.

Agnew, R., 2012. *Robert Agnew on Strain Theory and the American Society for Criminology* [Interview] (9 January 2012).

Agnew, R., 2016. Strain, Economic Status, and Crime. In: A. R. Piquero, ed. *The Handbook of Criminological Theory.* Oxford: John Wiley & Sons, Inc., pp. 209–229.

Agresti, A. & Finlay, B., 1997. *Statistical Methods for the Social Sciences.* 3rd Edition ed. New Jersey: Prentice-Hall International Inc.

Akers, R. L., 1998. *Social learning and social structure: a general theory of crime and deviance.* Boston: Northeastern University Press.

Akers, R. L. & Jennings, W. G., 2016. Social Learning Theory. In: A. R. Piquero, ed. *The Handbook of Criminological Theory*. Oxford: John Wiley & Sons, Inc., pp. 230–240.

Aller Maisonnave, G., 2016. ASPECTOS DOGMÁTICOS Y CRIMINOLÓGICOS DE LA DELINCUENCIA EMPRESARIAL. *Instituto Uruguayo de Derecho Penal*, Issue 2, pp. 1–17.

Basel Committee on Banking Supervision, 2005. *Compliance and the compliance function in banks*, Basel: Bank for International Settlements.

BBC News, UK, 2017. Grenfell Tower: Corporate manslaughter considered by police. *BBC*, 27 July.

Becker, H. S., 1963. *Outsiders: studies in the sociology of deviance.* New York: The Free Press.

Beck, U., 1992. *Risk Society: Towards a New Modernity.* London: SAGE Publications, Inc.

Bonger, W. A., 1969. *Criminality and economic conditions.* Bloomington(Indiana): Indiana University Press.

Bourdieu, P., 1977. *Outline of a Theory of Practice.* Cambridge: Cambridge University Press.

Braithwaite, J., 1985. White Collar Crime. *Annual Review of Sociology*, Volume 11, pp. 1–25.

Brewis, J. et al., 2017. *Introducing organizational behaviour and management.* Third edition ed. Andover (Hampshire): Cengage Learning EMEA.

Britt, C. L. & Rocque, M., 2016. Control as an Explanation of Crime and Delinquency. In: A. R. Piquero, ed. *The Handbook of Criminological Theory*. Oxford: John Wiley & Sons, Inc., pp. 182–208.

Bursik, R., 1988. Social disorganization and theories of crime and delinquency: problems and prospects. *Criminology*, November, 26(4), pp. 519–552.

CENDOJ, 2017. *Buscador: Resultados.* [Online] Available at: http://www.poderjudicial.es/search/indexAN.jsp [Accessed 1 08 2017].

Certo, S. T., 2003. Influencing Initial Public Offering Investors with Prestige: Signaling with Board Structures. *Academy of Management Review*, July, 28(3), pp. 432–446.

Clinard, M. B. & Quinney, R., 1973. *Criminal behavior systems: a typology.* 2nd Edition ed. New York: Holt, Rinehart and Winston.

Cohan, J. A., 2002. "I Didn't Know" and "I Was Only Doing My Job": Has Corporate Governance Careened out of Control? A Case Study of Enron's Information Myopia. *Journal of Business Ethics*, 40(3), pp. 275–299.

Cohen, M. A., 1996. Theories of Punishment and Empirical Trends in Corporate Criminal Sanctions. *Managerial and Decision Economics*, Volume 17, pp. 399–411.

Cohen, T., ed., 2001. *Jacques Derrida and the humanities: a critical reader.* New York: Cambridge University Press.

Colwell, S. R., Zyphur, M. J. & Schminke, M., 2011. When does Ethical Code Enforcement Matter in the Inter-Organizational Context? The Moderating Role of Switching Costs. *Journal of Business Ethics*, 104(1), pp. 47–58.

Cresswell, J. W. & Plano Clark, V. L., 2011. *Designing and conducting mixed method research.* 2nd Edition ed. Thousand Oaks: SAGE.

Davis, K., 1973. The Case for and Against Business Assumption of Social Responsibilities. *Academy of Management Journal*, 16(2), pp. 312–322.

Di Ronco, A., 2014. Multinational anti-corruption self-regulation in the pharmaceutical sector: evidence of (in)effectiveness. In: P. C. Van Duyne, et al. eds. *Corruption, greed and crime-money: sleaze and shady economy in Europe and beyond.* Oisterwijk: Wolf Legal Publishers, pp. 21–46.

Dodd, V. & Sherwood, H., 2017. Grenfell council 'may have committed corporate manslaughter'—Met police. *The Guardian*, 28 July.

Dolan, K. A. & Kroll, L., 2017. Forbes 2017 Billionaires List: Meet The Richest People On The Planet. *Forbes*, 20 March.

Donegan, J. J. & Ganon, M. W., 2008. Strain, Differential Association, and Coercion: Insights from the Criminology Literature on Causes of Accountant's Misconduct. *Accounting & the Public Interest*, Volume 8, pp. 1–20.

Eijsbouts, J., 2017. Corporate Codes as Private Co-Regulatory Instruments in Corporate Governance and Responsibility and Their Enforcement. *Indiana Journal of Global Legal Studies*, 24(1), pp. 181–205.

Enicov, I., 2016. Applying Game Theory In Risk Management. *Annals of the University of Oradea, Economic Science Series*, December, 25(2), pp. 283–291.

Epstein, C. F., 2010. The Contribution of Robert K. Merton to Culture Theory. In: C. J. Calhoun, ed. *Robert K. Merton: sociology of science and sociology as science.* New York: Columbia University Press, pp. 69–79.

Eser, A. & Burkhardt, B., 1995. *DERECHO PENAL Cuestiones fundamentales de la Teoría del Delito sobre la base de casos de sentencias.* 1st Edition ed. Madrid: Editorial Colex.

Federal Deposit Insurance Corporation, 2017. *Compliance Examination Manual*, Washington: FDIC.

Ferguson, G., 1999. The Basis for Criminal Responsibility of Collective Entities in Canada. In: A. Eser, G. Heine & B. Huber, eds. *Criminal Responsibility of Legal and Collective Entities International Colloquium Berlin, May 4–6, 1998.* Berlin: Freiburg im Breisgau, pp. 153–180.

Fleming, S., 2014. *The age of the compliance officer arrives.* [Online] Available at: https://www.ft.com/content/cadd54a6-c3bd-11e3-a8e0-00144feabdc0 [Accessed 05 2017].

Fletcher, G. P., 2000. *Rethinking Criminal Law.* New York: Oxford University Press, Inc.

Friedman, M., 1962. *Capitalism and Freedom.* 1982 Reissue ed. Chicago: The University of Chicago Press.

Friedman, M., 1970. The Social Responsibility of Business Is to Increase Its Profits. *The New York Times Magazine*, 13 September, pp. 173–178.

Friedrichs, D., 2017. Edwin H. Sutherland: An Improbable Criminological Key Thinker-For Critical Criminologists and for Mainstream Criminologists. *Critical Criminology*, March, 25(1), pp. 55–69.

G20, 2017. *High Level Principles on the Liability of Legal Persons for Corruption*, Hamburg: G20.

Gasiorowski-Denis, E., 2014. New ISO standard on compliance management cuts challenges and costs. *ISO News archive*, 19 December.

General Prosecutor's Office of Spain, 2016. *SOBRE LA RESPONSABILIDAD PENAL DE LAS PERSONAS JURÍDICAS CONFORME A LA REFORMA DEL CÓDIGO PENAL EFECTUADA POR LEY ORGÁNICA 1/2015*, Madrid: State Attorney.

Gobert, J. J. & Punch, M., 2003. *Rethinking corporate crime*. Bath: Butterworths.

Goff, C. & Geis, G., 2008. The Michael-Adler Report (1933): Criminology Under The Microscope. *Journal of the History of the Behavioral Sciences*, 44(4), pp. 350–363.

Goldstein, A. S. & Goldstein, J. eds., 1971. *Crime Law & Society*. New York: The Free Press.

Gottfredson, M. R. & Hirschi, T., 1990. *A general theory of crime*. Stanford(California): Stanford University Press.

Hagan, J., Gillis, A. R. & Simpson, J., 1985. The Class Structure of Gender and Delinquency: Toward a Power-Control Theory of Common Delinquent Behavior. *American Journal of Sociology*, 90(6), pp. 1151–1178.

Hertz Corp. v. Friend et al. (2010).

Heugens, P. & Oosterhout, J. v., 2008. Much ado about nothing: A conceptual critique of corporate social responsibility. In: D. Siegel, D. Matten, A. McWilliams & A. Crane, eds. *The Oxford Handbook of Corporate Social Responsibility*. Oxford: Oxford University Press, pp. 197–223.

Hirschi, T., 1977. Causes and Prevention of Juvenile Delinquency. *Sociological Inquiry*, July, 47(3–4), pp. 322–341.

Hoffmann, J. P., 2003. A Contextual Analysis of Differential Association, Social Control, and Strain Theories of Delinquency. *Social Forces*, 81(3), pp. 753–785.

Huck, J. L., Spraitz, J. D., Bowers Jr, J. H. & Morris, C. S., 2017. Connecting Opportunity and Strain to Understand Deviant Behavior: A Test of General Strain Theory. *Deviant Behavior*, 38(9), pp. 1009–1026.

International Organization for Standardization, 2010. *ISO 26000—Social responsibility*, Geneva: ISO.

International Organization for Standardization, 2014. *ISO 19600—Compliance management systems—Guidelines*, Geneva: ISO.

International Organization for Standardization, 2016. *ISO 37001—Anti-bribery management systems*, Geneva: ISO.

Interview 1, 2017. *1st. Participant* [Interview] (20 06 2017).

Interview 2, 2017. *2nd. Participant* [Interview] (20 06 2017).

Interview 3, 2017. *3rd. Participant* [Interview] (22 06 2017).

Interview 4, 2017. *4th. Participant* [Interview] (23 06 2017).

Interview 5, 2017. *5th. Participant* [Interview] (05 07 2017).

Interview 6, 2017. *6th. Participant* [Interview] (19 07 2017).

Jakobs, G., 1996. *La Imputación Objetiva en el Derecho Penal*. Buenos Aires: Ad-Hoc.

Jaques, E., 1951. *The changing culture of a factory.* London: Tavistock Publications.

Kant, I., 2012. *Groundwork of the metaphysics of morals.* Cambridge: Cambridge University Press.

Karasek, R. & Bryant, P., 2012. Signaling Theory: Past, Present, And Future. *Academy of Strategic Management Journal*, January, 11(1), pp. 91–99.

Karwacki, M., 2015. *The top five Spanish banks.* [Online] Available at: http://www.thebanker.com/Banker-Data/Bank-Trends/The-top-five-Spanish-banks?ct=true [Accessed 01 07 2017].

Kilmann, R., Saxton, M. & Serpa, R., 1985. Introduction: five key issues in understanding and changing culture. In: R. H. Kilmann, ed. *Gaining Control of the Corporate Culture.* San Francisco: Jossey-Bass, pp. 1–16.

Klinkhammer, J., 2013. On the dark side of the code: organizational challenges to an effective anti-corruption strategy. *Crime Law and Social Change*, 4 July, 60(2), pp. 191–208.

Knights, D. & Willmott, H., 2011. *Organizational analysis: essential readings.* Andover: South-Western Cengage Learning.

Krohn, M. D., 1999. Social Learning Theory: The Continuing Development of a Perspective. *Theoretical Criminology*, 1 November, 3(4), pp. 462–476.

Kubrin, C. E. & Wo, J. C., 2016. Social Disorganization Theory's Greatest Challenge: Linking Structural Characteristics to Crime in Socially Disorganized Communities. In: A. R. Piquero, ed. *The Handbook of Criminological Theory.* Oxford: John Wiley & Sons, Inc., pp. 121–136.

Lammers, C. & Hickson, D., 1979. *Organizations Alike and Unlike: International and Interinstitutional Studies in the Sociology of Organizations.* London: Routledge & Kegan Paul.

Langton, L. & Piquero, N. L., 2007. Can general strain theory explain white-collar crime? A preliminary investigation of the relationship between strain and select white-collar offenses. *Journal of Criminal Justice*, 35(1), pp. 1–15.

Laub, J. H., 2006. Edwin H. Sutherland And The Michael-Adler Report: Searching For The Soul Of Criminology Seventy Years Later. *Criminology*, May, 44(2), pp. 235–258.

Laufer, W. S., 2014. *Liability, Corporate Bodies and Guilty Minds: The Failure of Corporate Criminal.* Paperback edition 2008 ed. Chicago: University of Chicago Press.

Lavorgna, A. & Di Ronco, A., 2015. Codes of ethics in the Italian professional football. In: P. Van Duyne, et al. eds. *The Relativity of Wrongdoing: Corruption, Organised Crime, Fraud and Money Laundering in Perspective.* Oisterwijk: Wolf Legal Publishers, p. 253–282.

Logsdon, J. M. & Wood, D. J., 2002. Business Citizenship: From Domestic To Global Level Of Analysis. *Business Ethics Quarterly*, 12(2), pp. 155–187.

Luhmann, N., 1964. *Funktionen und Folgen formaler Organisation (Schriftenreihe der Hochschule Speyer).* Berlin: Duncker & Humblot.

Maramwidze-Merrison, E., 2016. Innovative Methodologies in Qualitative Research: Social Media Window for Accessing Organisational Elites for interviews. *Electronic Journal of Business Research Methods*, 14(2), pp. 157–167.

Mark, G. A., 1987. The Personification of the Business Corporation in American Law. *University of Chicago Law Review*, 54(4), pp. 1441–1483.

Markoff, G., 2012. Arthur Andersen and the Myth of the Corporate Death Penalty: Corporate Criminal Convictions in the Twenty-First Century. *University of Pennsylvania Journal of Business Law*, 15(3), pp. 797–842.

Martin, J., 1998. *Organizational Behaviour.* 1st Edition ed. London: International Thomson Business Press.

McFarland, D. A. & Gómez, C. J., 2014. Organizational Culture. In: *Organizational Analysis*. s.l.: Daniel A. McFarland, Charles J. Gomez, pp. 96–112.

Melé, D., 2009. Corporate Social Responsibility Theories. In: A. Crane, et al. eds. *The Oxford Handbook of Corporate Social Responsibility*. New York: Oxford University Press, pp. 47–82.

Merton, R. K., 1938. Social Structure and Anomie. *American Sociological Review*, 3(5), pp. 672–682.

Merton, R. K. & Nisbet, R. A., 1976. *Contemporary social problems*. 4th Edition ed. New York: Harcourt Brace Jovanovich.

Michalowski, R. J. & Kramer, R. C., 2006. *State-corporate crime: wrongdoing at the intersection of business and government*. New Brunswick: Rutgers University Press.

Mir Puig, S., 2005. *Derecho Penal Parte General*. 7th Edition ed. Barcelona: Editorial Reppertor.

OECD, 2015. *G20/OECD Principles of Corporate Governance*, Paris: OECD Publishing.

Oxford Dictionaries, 2017. *English Oxford Living Dictionaries*. [Online] Available at: https://en.oxforddictionaries.com/definition/citizen [Accessed 2017].

Palinkas, L. A. et al., 2013. Purposeful Sampling for Qualitative Data Collection and Analysis in Mixed Method Implementation Research. *Administration and Policy in Mental Health and Mental Health Services Research*, 6 November, 42(5), pp. 533–544.

Patton, M., 2002. *Qualitative research and evaluation methods*. Thousand Oaks (California): Sage Publications.

Rahim, M. M. & Alam, S., 2014. Convergence of Corporate Social Responsibility and Corporate Governance in Weak Economies: The Case of Bangladesh. *Journal of Business Ethics*, June, 121(4), pp. 607–620.

Res. 260/2017 (2017).

Res. No. 121/2017 (2017).

Res. No. 154/2016 (2016).

Res. No. 221/2016 (2016).

Res. No. 516/2016 (2016).

Rindova, V. P., Pollock, T. G. & Hayward, M. L. A., 2006. Celebrity Firms: The Social Construction of Market Popularity. *Academy of Management Review*, January, 31(1), pp. 50–71.

Robbins, S. P. & Judge, T. A., 2014. *Essentials of organizational behavior*. Twelfth edition ed. Harlow(Essex): Pearson.

Roxin, C., 1997. *Derecho Penal Parte General: Tomo I: Fundamentos. La Estructura de la Teoría del Delito*. Madrid: Civitas.

Said, R., Crowther, D. & Amran, A., 2014. Introduction: Corporate Crime and Its Constraint. In: R. Said, D. Crowther & A. Amran, eds. *Ethics, Governance and Corporate Crime: Challenges and Consequences*. Bingley: Emerald, pp. 1–18.

Sanchez, G. R. & Vargas, E. D., 2016. Taking a Closer Look at Group Identity: The Link between Theory and Measurement of Group Consciousness and Linked Fate. *Political Research Quarterly*, 1 March, 69(1), pp. 160–174.

Sarantakos, S., 2013. *Social Research*. 4th Edition ed. s.l.: Palgrave Macmillan.

Schelling, T. C., 2006. *Micromotives and Macrobehavior*. New York: W. W. Norton & Company, Inc.

Schnyder, G. & Kern, P., 2015. *Law and Agency: The micro-foundations of institutional change in national corporate governance systems*. [Online] Available at: https://discover.ukdataservice.ac.uk/catalogue/?sn=851977&type=Data%20catalogue [Accessed 04 06 2017].

Segre, S., 2014. *Contemporary Sociological Thinkers and Theories*. Farnham(Surrey): Ashgate.

Silva Sanchez, J.-M., 2016. *Fundamentos del Derecho Penal de la Empresa*. 2nd Edition ed. Madrid: Edisofer S.L.

Solomon, R. C., 1992. *Ethics and Excellence: Cooperation and Integrity in Business*. New York: Oxford University Press.

Spence, M., 1973. Job Market Signaling. *The Quarterly Journal of Economics*, 87(3), pp. 355–374.

Stein, R., 2013. The pull of the group: Conscious conflict and the involuntary tendency towards conformity. *Consciousness and Cognition*, September, 22(3), pp. 788–794.

Sutherland, E. H., 1940. White-Collar Criminality. *American Sociological Review*, February, 5(1), pp. 1–12.

Sutherland, E. H., 1944. Is "White Collar Crime" Crime?. *American Sociological Review*, 10(2), pp. 132–139.

Sutherland, E. H., 1983. *White Collar Crime: The Uncut Version*. Binghampton(New York): Yale University Press.

Tesco Supermarkets Ltd. v. Natrass (1971).

The Pervert's Guide To Ideology. 2012. [Film] Directed by Sophie Fiennes. United Kingdom: Blinder Films; British Film Institute (BFI); Film4; Irish Film Board; Neue Vitaskop Film; P Guide Productions; Rooks Nest Entertainment; Transmitter Film.

The Transnational institute, 2014. *Planet Earth: A Corporate World.* [Online] Available at: https://www.tni.org/en/infographic/planet-earth-corporate-world [Accessed 2017].

Thomas, G., 2016. *How To Do Your Case Study.* 2nd Edition ed. London: SAGE Publications Ltd.

Thyssen, O., 2009. *Business Ethics and Organizational Values. A systems-theoretical analysis.* Softcover reprint of the hardcover 1st edition ed. London: Palgrave Macmillan.

Tittle, C. R., 1995. *Control balance: toward a general theory of deviance.* Boulder: Westview Press.

Tombs, S. & Whyte, D., 2015. *The Corporate Criminal: why corporations must be abolished.* Abingdon(Oxfordshire): Routledge.

Trevino, L. K. & Weaver, G. R., 2001. Organizational Justice and Ethics Program "Follow-Through": Influences on Employees' Harmful And Helpful Behavior. *Business Ethics Quarterly*, October, 11(4), pp. 651–671.

United Nations, 2004. *UN Convention Against Corruption (UNCAC)*, New York: United Nations.

United Nations, 2011. *Guiding Principles on Business and Human Rights*, New York and Geneva: United Nations.

Wells, C., 1999. A New Offence of Corporate Killing—the English Law Commission's Proposals . In: A. Eser, G. Heine & B. Huber, eds. *Criminal Responsibility of Legal and Collective Entities International Colloquium Berlin, May 4–6, 1998.* Berlin: Freiburg im Breisgau, pp. 119–128.

Wells, C., 2001. *Corporations and Criminal Responsibility.* Second Edition ed. New York: Oxford University Press.

Wengraf, T., 2001. *Qualitative Research Interviewing.* 1st Edition ed. London: Sage.

Wolf, S., 1985. The legal and moral responsibility of organisations. In: R. Pennock & J. W. Chapman, eds. *Criminal Justice.* New York: New York University Press, pp. 267–288.

Wood, D. J., 1991. Corporate Social Performance Revisited. *Academy of Management Review*, 16(4), pp. 691–718.

Young, J., 1981. Thinking seriously about crime: some models of criminology. In: *Crime and Society: Readings in History and Theory.* London: Routledge, pp. 206–260.

Zaffaroni, E. R., 2013. Seeking the Enemy: From Satan to Cool Criminal Law. In: *Criminology and Criminal Policy Movements.* Lanham(Maryland): Rowman & Littlefield, pp. 5–33.

Zaffaroni, E. R., Alagia, A. & Slokar, A., 2002. *Derecho Penal Parte General.* 2nd Edition ed. Buenos Aires: Ediar.

www.ingramcontent.com/pod-product-compliance
Lightning Source LLC
Chambersburg PA
CBHW031334230926
51848CB00001B/224
9789004407732